Reaching Home Plate

An In-Depth Guide on Getting Recruited, Conquering Adversity, and Achieving Mastery

By

Perry Quartuccio

Disclaimer: All thoughts, views, and opinions, other than the contributors', are my own.

Dedication

To my family, my friends, and my loved ones… for supporting me throughout this writing process,

To my teachers and professors… for being my mentors and friends to help me with this book,

To the parents, players, and coaches reading this,

To Baseball.

Special Acknowledgements

Melissa Astarita- Content Design

Bobby Jenkins- Content Contributor

Jake Lawrie- Content Contributor

Kia Sabo- Cover Art, Layout, Content Design

Dianne Drewing- Content Contributor

Dr. Deborah Fish Ragin- Content Contributor

Linda Zani Thomas- Copy Consultation

These great people are the reason this book is even possible. I owe them all of my gratitude. Thank you for helping me, guiding me, and motivating me. I appreciate you tremendously.

Special Dedication

To my beautiful grandmother:

Florence "Dolly" Quartuccio

May your soul rest in peace.

I love you.

LINEUP

Introduction

Here I am, a clueless sophomore in college with no idea on what I want to do with my life. I'm in Dr. Rob Gilbert's Sports Psychology class and the first thing he says to our class is this: "My goal for this class is to try to inspire you to do one of two things. One: write your own book. Two: break a world record." Is this guy crazy? First day of classes and this guy standing in front of me is going to tell me he's going to inspire me to write a book or break a world record. Did he forget that he's talking to a bunch of college kids? After he said that, I shut him out. My mind wandered as I thought about fall baseball practice later that afternoon. What color are we wearing today? Red or black? I wonder if I'm pitching today. God, will this guy shut up already? I'm not writing a book, I'm 19 years old and I absolutely don't care about this world record that recorded how many saltine crackers a human being can eat in one minute.

Well, a couple months later, here I am. Writing a book. At age 20. I had a very general vision for this book. My only topics were RECRUITING, DEALING WITH ADVERSITY, and OVERALL ADVICE. I reached out to maybe ten people in regards to contributions to fulfill these topics, wrote maybe four pages, and then I didn't open up this document until about late March. As I'm writing this, the COVID-19 pandemic is still having a profound impact globally. We're all living in this unusual and different time, for this is something we've never experienced before. We're forced to adjust and adapt to this new world where all we can do is stay home, sit tight, and hope and pray in this time of pain and worry. We're all forced to stay strong and stay connected. My thoughts go out to those who are suffering terribly from this pandemic.

All organized and professional sports have been canceled for a little over two months now. I'm certain we're all losing our minds with the inability to watch sports. I can't imagine being a senior in high school, who may be still trying to get recruited. I can't imagine being a senior in college, who had to face the fact that their athletic career had ended abruptly, with no real sense of closure. My thoughts and prayers go out to all of those who had their season cut short.

As unfortunate and tragic as this pandemic is, it's important to find the positives within it all—perhaps it's finding a new hobby, catching up with old friends, or for me, writing this book. Do something different and find the positives. This book is **my** positive.

This entire book is everything I have learned while playing the beautiful sport of baseball for 15 years of my life. The successes, the tribulations, the ups, the downs—all of what baseball has given me.

This year, my last year of playing baseball, I made the decision to not to come out for my college team at the start of my sophomore season. I do not regret this decision.

I remember coming home from school one random weekend in January. At that point, I had not yet decided whether or not I wanted to return this year to play. We just got a new head coach, and he had plans for tryouts/practices the following week. He'd asked the team days before for preferred numbers for tryouts— I still had not texted him my numbers. January 16, 1:45 p.m. "Perry need your number choices." My heart sunk. I opened the front door, walked to my car and opened it. I sat in my car for 20 minutes rehearsing what I should say and how I should say it.

"Now, it's my turn to give back to baseball."

I called Coach, and my voice was raspy. I said hesitantly, "Coach, I think it's in my best interest not to try out for the team this year. I'm sorry." My breath started to get heavier, my eyes

started watering, but I had to hold back a torrential downpour of tears because I was still on the phone call. Coach and I talked for a solid ten minutes, in regards to my career and school goals, and then we hung up. Torrential downpour. I hung up my cleats.

Not playing baseball was the hardest decision of my life. I was letting go of something I had invested so much time and energy, not to mention money as well. Just weeks later, I realized that I wasn't giving up—I was moving on. I value this decision as a true milestone in my life— where I could place my time and energy into something other than baseball.

With that being said, it doesn't neglect the fact that baseball turned me into the person I am today. I believe that. Baseball gave me lifelong friendships and relationships. Baseball gave me discipline, a hard work-ethic, and a true understanding of what it means to be there for someone else, for a team. Baseball gave me a lesson on the importance of nutrition and exercise. You don't always get these lessons in a classroom or online, but through baseball, you get these unique experiences. Baseball has given me so much. Now, it's my turn to give back to baseball. It's my time to give back to the baseball community that has given me all of the tools I need to succeed in life going forward. This book is my paying it forward.

To all the walk-offs,

To all the strikeouts,

To all the championships,

To all the injuries,

To all the bus rides,

To all the practices,

To all the hotels,

To all the new gear,

To all of the memories,

To Baseball,

Thank you.

Reader's Note:

The initial version of this is an eBook.

This book's intention is to serve as a great resource for almost every aspect of the game, where I share my personal experiences and lessons. You also see the perspectives from all types of players, coaches, and other professionals mentioned. For most resources, I provide links to their websites, as well as include their social media handles. As much information as there may be in this book, it's up to you, the reader, to take everything with a grain of salt, soak it all up, and find what works best for you and/or your kid.

Bruce Lee said it best:

Adopted from Pixabay

"Absorb what is useful, discard what is useless and add what is specifically your own."

"From personal experience, growing up with a crazy baseball dad was not easy."

Youth Parents

This is something that needs to be addressed. **Less youths are playing sports because they feel too much pressure from their very own parents.** They lose interest too quick. Why? Because it's no longer about winning. Their interests are strictly making sure they perform well in front of their parents. Kids play to try to please them. They don't find winning fun. They find not being judged, criticized, or scrutinized to be very much fun. There's a fine line between constructive criticism and personal attack.

Youths look up to their parents. They value their opinion, their outlook on them, and never want to disappoint. Failing means disappointing. So maybe if they stop playing... they can stop failing... so they're never a disappointment to their parents again.

Overzealous parents instill this fixed mindset in their children. "If I don't succeed. I'm a failure." In Carol Dweck's *Mindset*, she explains perfectly how to NOT instill this fixed mindset in children, but to have them develop the growth mindset. The growth mindset doesn't encourage failure. It encourages learning through failure.

The growth mindset undoubtedly stems from parents. If your child does really well in his little league game, he goes 2-2 with a home run. Clearly, you (the parent) are happy, and your kid is happy. While successful games are great and necessary for maintaining interest, parents should not praise their kids' success so much, instead, parents should praise the hard work that allowed them to succeed. Parents should say something along the lines of, "All that extra practice worked out!" Don't praise the talent, praise the process. Emphasize development. With this mindset, youths can enjoy the rewarding feeling of actual hard work, as opposed to enjoying the rewarding feeling of not receiving harsh criticism from their parents.

Most people believe that the growth mindset simply rewards effort and participation. Effort is not hard. Participation is not hard. Rewarding participation does more harm than good, for it induces children to believe that they can be rewarded by just showing up. Awards that are earned through dedication and hard work should be encouraged, for that will provide their children with an adequate understanding of how to achieve anything they want not only in sports, but in life.

From personal experience, growing up with a crazy baseball dad was not easy. I, too, had a tremendous amount of pressure unnecessarily put on me. I was good, really good, at a young age and a lot was expected of me. I played on more travel teams than you can count on two hands. I have had every hitting and pitching coach in the world. I had the most updated version of every bat. I was the baseball prodigy in my family. All of this was fun, sure. I made a ton of friends, sure, but none of this mattered to me if I went 0-3 with 2 strikeouts. If I made an error on the field, I could already hear my dad's loud footsteps on the side.

The entire field heard him bang on the bleachers. The car ride home? Dreaded it. That was my dad.

Just about my sophomore year in high school, I told my dad I didn't really want him watching my games anymore. After having that difficult conversation, my dad came to the games, but he would watch by himself somewhere distant, probably somewhere in the outfield.

As I grew older, I think my dad understood my needs and started to realize the amount of pressure he thrust on me. I started to take my personal development into my own hands. My dad and I got even closer when we both mutually agreed on what our needs and wants were. Thank you, Dad, for allowing me to turn into the ballplayer I wanted to be, not what YOU wanted me to be.

Every parent wants to see their children succeed. Every parent wants what's best for their children. Unfortunately, most parents corrupt their youth's passion for sports, even if they think that what they're doing is for the better.

IN A NUTSHELL

- instill growth mindset

- encourage learning, process, development, etc.

- understand what your kid needs (not what you need/want)

- do not award participation

Content created By Perry Quartuccio

Rob Friedman- AKA "The Pitching Ninja"- MLB & ESPN Pitching Contributing Analyst

All baseball fans and players are familiar with that guy on Twitter who posts the awesome gifs of pitchers, right? That guy is Rob Friedman, AKA "The Pitching Ninja". He has an incredibly useful Twitter thread involving youths and their development. Thank you, Rob, for allowing me to share this!

Rob tweeted this thread that parents and coaches should be aware of for youths:

Steve Springer- Performance Coach & Major League Scout for Toronto Blue Jays. Former Professional Player for 14 years

ON YOUTH SPORTS

"Don't let your kids quit! If it's not fun, they will quit. Kids usually quit at age 13 because of the pressure that is put on them by the ones that love them the most (us parents) and Johnny testosterone coach yelling at my 10-year-old. Here are a few tips on how to stop youths from quitting a sport."

- Stay on your kids to get good grades.

- Make practices FUN.

- Get parents involved.

- Make it competitive

- Have different groups/stations.

- Don't yell at kids from age <12. Yelling at this age is not coaching them. It's simply humiliating them in front of their peers.

Twitter: @qualityatbats Instagram: @qualityatbats

Coach/Player Relationships

Photo Adopted from Pixabay

This chapter consists of a brief introduction from Steve Springer, followed by three videos explaining what a good coach/player relationship should look like. These videos are **amazing**. I'm truly inspired by these guys and I hope that I can be there for any player that I may coach in the future.

Steve Springer

The most important thing you need to know is this:

BASEBALL IS THE #1 MOST SELF-ESTEEM DESTROYING SPORT IN THE WORLD

"I don't need my coach, parent, or teammate to beat me up. The game is going to do it by itself."

COACHES TIP:

Players have to know that you care about them before they can care about what you know.

        ✓ Build them up

        ✓ Break them down with coaching

        ✓ Build them up again

Tim DeJohn- MiLB Fielding Coach- Baltimore Orioles

Tim and I had a really great conversation on the coach/player relationship. He is mainly the reason this chapter even exists. Listen to what Tim has to say! This is a MUST WATCH.

https://youtu.be/LHPlab6LGBM (Watch on YouTube Channel)

That is what a GREAT coach looks like. I believe 'DJ' (Tim's nickname on the ballfield) will have a coaching career for a very long time.

Twitter: @DeJohn_5 Instagram: @dejohn_5

Cale Hennemann- Assistant Coach- Belmont University

Cale played under DJ at the University of Memphis. Here's what he has to say on the importance of a solid coach/player relationship.

https://youtu.be/bow5qv3T19g (Watch on YouTube Channel)

Twitter: @CaleHennemann Instagram: @CaleHennemann

20

TJ Ward- Assistant Coach- Ramapo College

TJ played under DJ at the University of Hartford. Here's what he has to say about DJ, and how their relationship helped him as a player and now as a coach.

https://youtu.be/ DY_WCzCbXNY (Watch on YouTube Channel)

Twitter: @tj_ward3 Instagram: @t3swings

This entire section is located on my YouTube page. The YouTube channel is called "Reaching Home Plate". These videos are a 'must watch' for anyone trying to grasp a true understanding of what a coach/player relationship should look like.

Getting Recruited

My take on recruiting is this: stick out! For the most part, the recruiting process is tedious and stressful. The best thing you can do to get recruited by a college is to make yourself be noticed. This is easier said than done. There are many ways to get recognized by recruiters in all types of different sports. Your athletic ability on the field is single handedly the most important thing a college recruiter notices. For baseball, it's usually the measurables that initially make you stick out. By measurables, I mean your velocity, your exit velocity, etc. That's not the only thing a coach looks for though. Once they see that talent, that raw ability of you playing the game—they look at the small things. How are your grades? How do you act outside of competition? How is your mental game? How do you respond to failure? The mental aspect of any sport is highly overlooked when it comes to recruiting. It is easy to tell as a recruiting coordinator that a kid has bad body language, a bad attitude, or a bad mindset.

I read a book in the fall of 2018 that I wish I read when I was going to college camps and was trying to get recruited. It's a book by Harvard professor Amy Cuddy, *Presence*. She essentially said that we (human beings) don't just fear opportunity. We fear a future that hasn't even occurred to us. We all do that. Not just us baseball players. Everyone does that. We, along with the rest of the world, can own up to being in a future full of opportunity — but we dread it. We dread this unknown, monstrous, and scary future that hasn't even happened yet— whether that be asking someone out on a date, preparing for SATs, or trying to get recruited at a college camp or showcase. How does the human mind create these falsified futures? Cuddy suggests that the next time we feel anxious about an opportunity, we must approach it with **confidence** and **excitement**. That brings me to my last tip of getting recruited. Be confident. Confidence is firmly believing and trusting your own abilities. Get the opportunity. Visualize your goal. Own and trust your ability. And go get it!

Numerous college players and coaches, as well as some professional players share their insights on the recruiting process. Here's my experience.

MY RECRUITING STORY

My recruiting story is pretty simple. It was the summer of my junior year in high school and I was extremely passionate to play baseball in college, even after my horrible spring season. At this time, I was emailing coaches, playing in showcase tournaments, and attending schools' camps. At one camp in particular, at Montclair State University, I performed really well. Camps were not all that scary to me; a majority of camps, if not all, are moneymakers. Every camp in which I participated, I went in there with no regrets or holding back. I knew if I was going to get noticed, I had to stick out because there are hundreds of other kids who are trying to do the same thing as me. The thing I had on those kids was that I wasn't nervous and I never wavered. At the Montclair State camp, I struck out the first three kids on 10 pitches. The next two batters I managed to get out on weak contact. I felt invincible. After my performance, the coach asked me if I could return to the other camp that they were hosting the next week. This was clearly a great sign. When I returned the next week, I pitched decent, definitely not better than my first go-around. I guess that didn't have much of an impact due to the fact that I stood out in the first camp. I must've proved to be consistent and composed as a pitcher for another five batters. I threw to 10 batters, topping out at nearly 79 MPH. I was offered a visit.

On the visit, I was offered a roster spot and it took me about a week to decide I was going to commit there. An important aspect for me was the academics of the university. I'm a big advocate for choosing a school that is a fit for an individual. That is so cliché and basic to say but, in my opinion, I was not going to commit to Montclair State if it didn't have the major that I was interested in and if it was too far from home. These factors were important to me and luckily, Montclair has a great psychology program and it's a little more than an hour drive away from home. Before this point in my life, I knew I was not going to play at a Division I school, so I attended the Division III camps around New Jersey. This brings me to my next topic of discussion.

College baseball is college baseball. No matter what Division or level. Parents and kids have this preconceived notion that if it's not Division I baseball, then it's 'not good enough' and there's no way to get drafted out of Division II, III, or other JUCO colleges. This is the furthest from the truth. Anyone can get noticed and anyone can get drafted. I think that this is topic is dying down, since we have been seeing a tremendous number of players signing professional contracts out of the DII and DIII schools. Heck, all you have to do is post a video online and you can get noticed! Just because you play baseball on a level that isn't Division I does not mean you suck. Please get this out of your heads.

Looking back, **I wish I spent a little less time playing at showcases** and **more time on developing elite level skills**. This is one of my biggest regrets, something that comes to my attention on a daily basis — if I spent more time in the weight room or on the field perfecting my craft, would I have gone to a Division I school? Would I have gotten drafted? Would I still be playing? These questions remain unanswered.

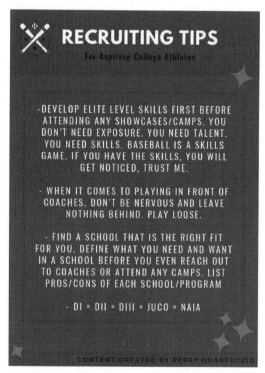

RECRUITING TIPS

For Aspiring College Athletes

-DEVELOP ELITE LEVEL SKILLS FIRST BEFORE ATTENDING ANY SHOWCASES/CAMPS. YOU DON'T NEED EXPOSURE. YOU NEED TALENT. YOU NEED SKILLS. BASEBALL IS A SKILLS GAME. IF YOU HAVE THE SKILLS, YOU WILL GET NOTICED, TRUST ME.

- WHEN IT COMES TO PLAYING IN FRONT OF COACHES, DON'T BE NERVOUS AND LEAVE NOTHING BEHIND. PLAY LOOSE.

- FIND A SCHOOL THAT IS THE RIGHT FIT FOR YOU. DEFINE WHAT YOU NEED AND WANT IN A SCHOOL BEFORE YOU EVEN REACH OUT TO COACHES OR ATTEND ANY CAMPS. LIST PROS/CONS OF EACH SCHOOL/PROGRAM

- DI = DII = DIII = JUCO = NAIA

CONTENT CREATED BY PERRY QUARTUCCIO

Let's take a look at the perspectives of other college players and coaches:

Hayden Wesneski- New York Yankees Organization RHP

I think the best way to get recruited is to go to their recruiting camp. They see you in person and you get to meet the coaches. If you can't do that, you (the athlete), not your mom or dad, should email the college expressing your interest in their program. Talk about you as a person and baseball player. The coach is not only getting a baseball player, but a human being.

Matt Barnes- Shenandoah University RHP

Be persistent. Always be on a coach's mind. Email coaches about coming to games, tournaments, showcases— anything where you can show yourself off. Email them stats and about games. Email them videos.

Victor Diaz- Assistant Baseball Coach- Embry-Riddle Aeronautical University

First and foremost, when it comes to recruiting, we are looking for the needs of our team and the best fit for our university and program. I think the fit of an athlete depends on what type of University you are coaching at and what type of player will fit with the type of team you are trying to build. The initial things I personally look for other than skill set and ability are maturity and personality. Will this be an athlete that is enjoyable to be around? Is the athlete responsible? Is he reaching out on his own and asking good questions?

Best advice to an athlete in the recruiting process is to be a great communicator. Many coaches have a lot on their plates on top of balancing work and family life. Don't expect for the coach to continue to keep tabs on you. Make an effort to initiate communication and show the coach you have a genuine interest in the program and university.

Tommy Winterstein- Assistant Baseball Coach- University of Toledo

Outside of talent level, we try to look at what might separate one guy from the other. To me, character and work ethic are huge as well as being able to deal with adversity. In life and in baseball, we are going to face adversity at some point. It is inevitable, but how a guy can respond to that is where a guy may take leaps and bounds as far as his personal and athletic development. Going back to my first point, this is why character and work ethic are huge! I would say to an athlete looking to be recruited: stay open minded. You might have your sights set on one thing but don't get lost in the pursuit of that and get tunnel vision and miss what could be a great opportunity somewhere else.

George Capen- Assistant Baseball Coach/ Recruiting Coordinator- The College of the Holy Cross

"I firmly believe that there is a school for every player if they want it bad enough and look hard enough."

When I'm out on the road recruiting, I look for raw athleticism above anything else. I want to see how his actions are, how his hand-eye coordination is, how his feet move, etc. Nothing is more valuable to me as a coach. We don't recruit to fill positions (with the exception of pitchers and catchers). We are looking to bring in the best available **athletes**, regardless of position. A kid with the natural ability to have a feel for his body is going to be able to make adjustments significantly quicker, whether that be on the mound, behind the dish, out in the field, or in the box. That's why I value the movements more than anything.

Oftentimes, you can get a preliminary evaluation on his athleticism just during his catch play.

The most important thing athletes can do during the recruiting process is be themselves. This means writing your own emails to schools, being honest about your current skill set, and presenting yourself in a way that you will be able to back up with your actions once you arrive on campus. I firmly believe that there is a school for every player if they want it bad enough and look hard enough. So, it all comes down to finding the right fit for both the player and the school and that is only going to become apparent when both sides are **transparent** and **honest** about who they are and what they are looking for.

Richard Croushore- Pitching Coach- Shenandoah University- Former 11 Year MLB Veteran

I am looking for athleticism no matter what positions they play. If they have athletic feel and talent, I have found that they can learn the pieces needed to get better at a specific part of the game. I also talk to a recruit's coach about their competitiveness, work ethic, leadership skills, and personality. I try to stay away from the "prima donnas" no matter how good they are. I also consider the kind of student they are. If they are lazy in the classroom, they will be lazy on the field. Dummies are hard to coach!

Be available to be seen...whether it is a good summer team or a recruiting service showcase. Also, play hard and hustle at all times and, by all means, keep your head right no matter how good or bad it's going.

Joe Duffy- University of Sciences OF

The recruiting process can be a daunting task for any baseball player looking to play in college. Plenty of current and former college baseball players have regrets about their own recruiting process. It's not easy. It is important to know and understand how the process works as early as possible. The process can begin as early as a player's freshman year of high school. The latest a player should start is the summer following his junior year. There are four main parts of the recruiting process:

1. Making a list of schools

2. Ranking your list

3. Selling yourself to coaches

4. Making the decision

As early as possible, you want to make a list of schools you are interested in based on everything that **isn't** baseball related. This is the exact same process a student would go through as if they were just looking for a college to attend. Note everything that is important to you in a school, whether it be campus size, location, or maybe whether a school has a good football team. It's also important not to limit your list to just Division 1 schools. There are plenty of good baseball programs and good schools outside of Division 1. It might come to a point where you may not have any offers from Division 1 schools. Plus, going to a non-Division 1 school may be better for some players because they may get more playing time throughout their four years. You can always add or take away schools from your list at any time.

It's then time to rank the schools on your list. There are two parts to ranking schools. The first part can be done before a coach ever sees you play and the second part comes further down the line, if and when a school shows interest in you. There are some things you can't know without visiting the school or going to see the team play. First, you want to rank the schools based on things you can find out at home. You can rank them on any basis you want to, but there are definitely things you should keep in mind. There are some factors that are baseball-related that are important to think about. Look to see how well a team does in its conference. It's far more enjoyable to play for a team that competes for conference championships and regionals no matter what division the school is in. Look at roster size. Some schools have way too many players on their roster, meaning a lot don't play, so many will consider transferring out. You can then adjust your rankings as you find out more information.

The most important part of the recruiting process is selling yourself. You have to convince coaches that they want you on their roster. Make sure to find out the head coach and recruiting coordinator's email addresses online of all the schools on your list. You should make a resume with any videos, stats, and references you have to send to the coaches on your list. There are organizations and websites that help athletes display this information. Email the head coaches and the recruiting coordinators and introduce yourself. Mention your height, weight, position, and any notable attributes. Link your resume and make sure to show them your videos. Coaches love to see videos, so try to get as many videos of yourself playing or in the cages as much as possible. Coaches are going to want to see you play in person as well. Make sure to let them know when you are going to be playing in a tournament as they might be there and want to see you. If you sign up for a showcase that they are going to, send an email and let that coach know. Whenever you get a chance, introduce yourself in person. **Coaches like to match a face to a name.** Make sure to always be respectful. If coaches show interest in you, always make sure to respond to emails quickly.

If a coach is really interested, they will probably offer you a visit. When you're on a visit, be sure to talk to the players about the team. Ask them if it's enjoyable and if they like the coaches. Some may just tell you what you want to hear, but a lot of players will be honest with you. Again, be respectful, have a good time, and definitely ask questions.

Hopefully, you'll acquire some offers. Don't take any offers for granted. The best time to commit to a school is probably the summer after your junior year of high school. If you get a good offer from a school at the top of your list, you should probably take it no matter where in the process you are. Just remember that a lot of college coaches usually don't last too long at a single job. So, if the coach that recruited you either leaves or gets fired before you get there, you may be in a tough situation. That's another reason why it's important to find schools that do well in their conference because those coaches typically keep their jobs longer. If you have a decision between a few schools, go with your gut feeling. Find out as much information as you can about each one to help make your final decision. If you need to, a pros/cons list is a great way to see everything you like and dislike about a certain school. You can always reach out on social media to players on the team and ask them any questions you have at this point.

There's always the possibility that you don't get the offers that you want or any at all by the time decision day comes. There are still a few options. A great route to consider is the JUCO route. A lot of great players have come from junior college two-year schools. Teams are always looking for JUCO players to recruit because they are two years more experienced than kids coming out of high school. If you're an underdeveloped player, maybe you need to bulk up a bit, then this may be a great route for you. There are a lot of great coaches at

JUCO schools who really care about improving you as a player and getting you to the college you deserve to go to. If that's not for you, you can go back to your list and look at the schools at the top. You can always go to a school you know you'll like regardless of baseball and try to walk on the team. Teams will always allow players to try out and a lot of the times they'll take walk-ons just to have on the roster. A last resort for playing baseball in college is playing for the club team at one of the schools you want to go to. There are some schools with very competitive club baseball teams, which allows you to still play baseball and have some more time on your hands to enjoy college.

The recruiting process can be tough, but if you work hard and have a plan, you'll get somewhere you will enjoy being. It's important to remember that college is about having a good time and getting a good degree. Not many players end up making it to the major leagues, so you'll always want to have a good time while you're going on your journey with baseball. Another thing to keep in mind is to **be careful what you post on social media**. A coach will always be looking for a reason not to offer you. Always hustle on and off the field, show that you're a team player and play confidently. If you commit to a school, be aware that the school can always pull your offer at any point up until signing day, so **stay out of trouble**.

Pat Reilly- Vanderbilt University Commit RHP

My recruiting process went a lot differently than most. After my sophomore year of high school, I had only pitched about one varsity inning and summer ball was starting up. I recorded one bullpen and that's when everything took off. Getting good video from behind home plate or behind the mound can be so valuable. Two clips were uploaded to a recruiting website and I was receiving phone calls from dozens of college coaches. After having many fruitful conversations with coaches, I ended up committing to Northeastern, a DI program located in Boston, Massachusetts. I thought my recruiting process was over.

As a future Division I baseball player who has gone through the recruiting process, it is so important nowadays to use the technology we have to the best of our ability. There are a bunch of recruiting websites that hundreds of college coaches are on, such as NCSA or SportsRecruits. Another thing to do: post your bullpens to @Flatgroundapps on Twitter! These are so helpful: uploading video, sending stats or your schedule, or just sending regular emails to get your name in front of that coach. Do not only show a coach that you are a good player but show them you are a good person, too, someone who they would want on their team. There are so many little things that go into the process, and it almost all falls under having good communication skills. Being offered a scholarship is a coach's and school's investment into you. If you are not a well-rounded person, the investment will not be worth it for these schools and coaches. In this process, there is a lot that can be controlled outside of the game. As a player and a recruit, control what you can and communicate well.

In October of 2019, I had been committed for a year and was playing in my last travel ball game ever. That last game, I caught the eye of the pitching coach from Vanderbilt University and a few other 'big time' schools. About a week later I de-committed from Northeastern and was on a flight to Nashville to visit Vanderbilt's campus. Never in a million years would I have imagined myself in that spot. Recruiting is very weird. It never really ends. Someone is always watching, and it only takes one person, coach, or scout to absolutely change your world and give you an opportunity. As a player, I would say to work hard and enjoy the day-to-day process. There are only so many games in a year and only a few of those games will have college coaches watching. Make an impact. Do all the right things.

Conquering Adversity

"My senior year (HS). 0 innings. Let's discuss."

Adopted from www.montclairathletics.com

41

PERRY QUARTUCCIO

POSITION: Pitcher

HEIGHT: 5-8

WEIGHT: 185

CLASS: Freshman

HOMETOWN: Howell, NJ

HIGH SCHOOL: Christian Brothers Academy

💬 BIO 📖 RELATED 📊 STATS

2019 SEASON: Did not appear in any games.

MY STORY: THE YIPS→ "Did not appear in any games."

I have dealt with a tremendous amount of adversity—dealing with problems at home, to riding the bench, and to failing when I got the opportunities.

My junior year of high school is when I started to **crumble**. I'm not entirely sure what happened to my mechanics, my body, or my ability to pitch and throw strikes. I was self-diagnosed with this horrible disease called the "Yips". Those who know baseball, know what the yips is. It's essentially the sudden loss of baseball skill— as if you've never played the game before and you've become extraordinarily inexperienced. I could not throw a strike to save my life. The yips are not taken lightly either, it's a very sensitive topic for many players even to this day. People lose their dreams because of this sudden mental mystery that happens to baseball players. It's truly heartbreaking. Anyway, I don't remember how many innings I had my junior year, but it was definitely in the single digits. I never got out of a single inning either. I either walked the bases loaded or I threw 65 mph meatballs over the plate because I was too **afraid** to actually pitch.

My senior year. 0 innings. Let's discuss. The summer of my junior year, I pitched well. I was starting every weekend, throwing 5+ innings, letting up only 0-2 runs every game. Weird? Perhaps I had the seasonal yips. I regained my confidence on the mound and worked incredibly hard to get some innings back my senior year and prove myself. I also needed to step up my game, especially if I wanted to get recruited into a college.

Going into that spring, I threw decent in the early practices/tryouts. The coaches were surprised I could throw strikes again, as was I. After the team was finalized, we were getting ready to go to Florida for a spring break trip. During the trip, I finally got my opportunity to redeem myself as a dominant pitcher and show out in the spring season. Guess what happened again?! I was throwing balls in the dirt at about 56 ft. Wow I felt great, walking the ballpark in the simmering heat of Florida. This is awesome. I somehow got out of my first inning and barely sat down because our offense went 1-2-3. I threw my 5 warmup pitches and on the 5th pitch... my catcher gets up and throws an absolute pellet straight to the side of my skull, I go down, the crowd gasps in silence, the ball never got to second base. I couldn't catch a break. After many phone calls with my mom, a trip to the hospital, and many meetings with my coaches, I ended up having no concussion and I was cleared to play. After being cleared, I asked coach if I could pitch the next day and he reluctantly gave me the nod. The next morning, we had a game: I got absolutely shelled. There went my senior season.

In my first year of college, I threw 16 balls in a row in a fall scrimmage game. Do you know how hard it is to walk 4 guys in a row? I didn't just "deal" with adversity. I had to live with it; it's all I'd known— from my last two years of high school to my very short college career. For me, to not throw a single inning in two spring seasons had taken a toll on me mentally. However, that didn't stop me from showing up to practice every day and giving it 100%. That didn't stop me from working harder than everyone else in drill work, lifts, or running. I may not have been the best pitcher on the team, but I was undoubtedly one of the most dedicated players on our team. I take pride in that.

The thing I learned from not playing was simply this: everybody has a role on a team. Legendary coach Augie Garrido attested to this idea in his book *Life is Yours to Win*. Knowing my role and being the best teammate that I could be made me a better student and an even better person. That's how I **dealt** with adversity.

It's always been of interest to me to know how other people deal with adversity too.

Here's a look:

Hayden Wesneski

"The best baseball players have short memory."

The best way to deal with adversity is to stop looking at results. What I mean by that is don't look at the stats and have them tell you if you performed well or not. First, look at how you prepared. Then, you look and evaluate if you executed that plan. If you did both of those things, then you just tip your hat. You cannot control anything else. You learn from it and then forget. The best baseball players have short memory.

Josh Tols- Philadelphia Phillies Organization LHP

Off the field: For me, a solid routine is vital. If I know I have put in the work and followed my routine, it is much easier to deal with adversity when it arises. There are a lot of uncontrollable factors in baseball, so maintaining focus on what you can control is important.

In game: for me having a solid "reset" plan helps a lot. I like to take a deep diaphragmatic breath and then a quick full-body clench or flex. This often helps me reset my focus for the next batter. I have also found focusing on a specific rock or mark on the mound before getting signs is also a great reset.

It's important to learn from adversity and then move on. Baseball is a game of failure, but losing/failing/ adversity often teaches you lessons on how you can succeed in the future. Talk about it if you need to, but try not to dwell on it and let it affect you the next at bat, inning, or game.

Nick Cassano- Montclair State University IF

"Embrace adversity."

In life, how you handle adversity can make or break you. In the sport of baseball, it's no different. As baseball players we deal with adversity every single day, practice, game etc. Take such a simple example of adjusting to a 12-6 breaking ball when you were sitting dead-red fastball in a 3-2 count (we've all been there). Are you going to watch that curveball float over the dish into the strike zone? Or are you going to keep your weight back, double tap, and foul that sucker off and wait for your pitch? Baseball teaches you how to overcome adversity and how to embrace it, rather than wishing it never happened. Baseball teaches you to control what you can control. Yes, some people struggle with adversity— but some people struggle with going down looking, too. They'll come into the dugout and think of every excuse in the book as to why they K'ed up: "I wasn't expecting that." Well, life throws a lot of unexpected things your way. Instead of complaining, wondering why things happen, and feeling sorry for yourself, embrace what's thrown at you, learn how to fight it, and learn how to take it over the left field wall. Embrace adversity. Develop a plan. So, in your next at bat you know what to do when the pitcher throws you that 12-6. 'Cause in life, adversity happens more than once: be prepared for it, just like you are prepared for that breaking ball.

Jake Lawrie- Marist College Baseball LHP

I deal with adversity because I just have to. Adversity is an inevitable circumstance and if you love something enough it will just be a part of the process. You need to keep the bigger picture in mind and make yourself believe it is possible.

Brad Case- Pittsburgh Pirates Organization RHP

Whenever things get tough, I tell myself, "I just have to put my head down, and do the work." The tedious work to better myself every day can bring a lot of ease to my mind. The more and more I drill myself through something, the quicker the hard times seem to end.

Gary Trottier- Pitching Coach & Recruiting Coordinator- Lasell University

When I played in college, I dealt with adversity in a multitude of ways. For a majority of the time, I didn't handle it very well. I thought I did, but getting tough, mad, and beating my chest did nothing. When I finally learned how to deal with adversity was my senior year. I took everything for what it was, and immersed myself in every moment. I knew my time was ticking, and I didn't want to spend one inning of my last year being upset. It was my last year of meaningful baseball. How I embraced failure was quite simple. I'd ask myself these questions: Did I try my best? Did I prepare to the best of my ability? If I don't perform well, will I lose my house, degree, job, girlfriend, family? No. Once I checked everything off, I knew it was out of my control and embraced everything.

Twitter: @coachtrott Instagram: @coachtrott

Coach Victor Diaz

"It's either an obstacle or an opportunity."

I played Division 1 baseball at Mississippi State then transferred to State College of Florida, and back to Division 1 at Old Dominion. I went through many struggles and adversity. I had to overcome two arm surgeries. The way I dealt with it was growing as a person and learning how to bring value to my team in different ways. I also leaned on the confidence in my skill set and my goal of making an impact on my team. My teammates helped me get through a lot and I worked hard and stayed disciplined in my recovery so that I could make an impact on the field. Adversity is inevitable; it's going to happen. We have to learn to accept failure and understand it is going to happen whether we like it or not. It comes down to how we look at it. It's either an obstacle or an opportunity. I continued to look at adversity as an opportunity to grow and become better. Fortunately, it worked out and I had a successful career. I credit a lot of that success to my family, coaches, teammates, and friends. Adversity can be a lonely road but when you have a support system to lean on, it makes it a whole lot easier.

Coach George Capen

"Dealing with adversity is all about confidence."

To me, dealing with adversity is all about confidence. The more confidence you have, the quicker you are able to flush whatever mishaps come your way. You're able to move forward. I believe that confidence is only bred through being comfortable with failure and not being afraid of it. At the end of the road of the fear of failure is confidence. That's why baseball is such a great game to teach life lessons. It is a game of failure. It teaches you how to fail but, more importantly, how to overcome that adversity as quickly as possible. Adversity is inevitable and often might not be in your control. However, you can control your mentality through it all.

Coach Tommy Winterstein

"The journey is the reward."

One phrase that personally helped me deal with adversity was "the journey is the reward." Sometimes we get so lost in the final outcome that we are seeking that we forget to enjoy the journey and the process. When times get tough, you just have to remember your "why" and the most important part of that is surrounding yourself with people that share and understand your goals.

Gianluca Dalatri- UNC Chapel Hill RHP

"Throughout my baseball career, I was handed a few tough breaks—things that were far out of my control. Adversity in my career has been injuries, but more importantly, what the injuries have brought about in me mentally. Falling behind year after year through my injuries, I became obsessed with getting back to where I was. After year in and year out of dealing with injuries and continually falling behind, it only got worse. I began to change the way I went about thinking about each day at the field.

I learned that I couldn't make my day be all about baseball. It can only be **part** of my day. I started splitting my days up into three segments: class, stadium, night. What I'm challenging myself to do now is to limit baseball to the stadium. At that time, and ONLY at that time, my baseball mind is turned on. I work out, do my rehab, lift, throw, practice, watch video, and anything else you could imagine. I do everything possible to make the most of THAT day. Once I have accomplished what I need to get done, I go back into the locker room, grab my journal, and recap the things I did well and did not do well. I also write down my thoughts, my mood, and what I think I got better at. Once I'm done, I close the journal and tuck it away in my locker. I then shower, get changed, and leave. Once I step foot outside of the stadium, I tell myself that I am not allowed to think, focus, work on, or practice anything baseball-related until the next day. What this allows me to do is just focus on the rest of my day—whether that be going home to do work for class or just hang out with my best friends. Whatever I do, it doesn't matter. I consume myself at that moment. This has also allowed me to look forward to baseball and going to the field. Now, when I go to the field, I go with a purpose and excitement to work on things I've been itching to do for the past 24 hours. The biggest thing this idea of splitting my days into these three segments has done for me is that it has finally allowed me to **live in the moment**. I am able to enjoy what I am doing **now**. Not what I was doing or something I could be doing, but what I am currently doing at the moment and not letting anything else get in the way. In my opinion, the only way to be truly happy is to allow yourself to live in the present moment. The only way this is possible is if you allow yourself to let go of something you may be worried about that really has no meaning in your life in the grand scheme of things. Being truly happy is being able to consume yourself into what you are doing every moment and not worrying about the future or what may happen.

It is okay for adversity to shake us to our core. It is not supposed to be something that is easy to go through. The true marker of who we are as competitors is how we respond to the hand we have been dealt. How are we going to turn the negative experiences into positive results going forward? It is different for everyone. However, all that matters is that we figure out what each of us need to keep moving forward. At the end of the day, that is the true testament of our character."

Performance
Training

✓ Mental Performance

✓ Strength & Conditioning

✓ Mobility

✓ Pitching

✓ Hitting

✓ Fielding- Catching, Infield, Outfield

This next section consists of trainers, coaches, and specialists who devote their time and energy into players who want to get better. These guys are the best of the best. With their response page(s), I made sure to include their social media handles and/or websites for readers to link to if they like what a person or player said specifically. This book is about learning and development. Take it all in.

Mental Performance

WHAT IS MENTAL PERFORMANCE REALLY ABOUT?

- Enhances physical performance under pressure or stress
- Having more confidence
- Dealing with adversity
- Establishing sport-life balance
- What are your personal Values and what Culture are you around?

MENTAL SKILLS

- Goal setting
- Relaxation
- Growth Mindset
- Presence
- Visualization and Imagery
- Breathing
- Self awareness/Mindfulness
- Pre and post performance routines
- Leadership

CONTENT CREATED BY
PERRY QUARTUCCIO

Mental Performance is a Skillset

Mental performance training is something that tends to be overlooked in baseball. A common misconception is that mental performance is about being a "tough guy". Mental performance is more than just being inspired, watching motivational videos, and listening to "hype" music before a game. I have had very fruitful and enriching conversations with mental skills coaches in professional baseball who have pointed out to me that mental performance is a **skillset**.

It's something that needs to be practiced on a day to day basis. If you work out every day of the week, you expect to get in better shape, right? What's the difference for mental performance training? If you don't spend any time working on your mental performance, how do you expect your mental toughness, your grit, and your resiliency to show up when the game is on the line?

All of these questions—this entire perspective of mental performance training, made me realize that I definitely should have focused more on getting my mind right. Maybe I'd still be in the game if I did so. Lots of players, including myself, did not value the importance of mental performance and it's now something we regret and wish we had focused on more.

Grit/Resilience

If you want to learn about grit, read Angela Duckworth's *Grit*. Duckworth provides a true understanding of what grit is and why it is important. She also provides this "Grit Scale", a test that shows how gritty you are. This is important and most certainly applicable to all types of high performers, not just baseball athletes. Grit and resilience, two terms that seem to be coined together, are essentially what keep many elite performers from giving up on their long-term goals—even after being hit with adversity, injuries, or other setbacks. Grit is composed of two things: perseverance and passion, according to Duckworth (2016). The ability to respond to adversity is a gift of its own and it's always interesting to see how people respond differently (see "Conquering Adversity"). Another thing that I took from Duckworth's *Grit* are the two equations she discovered when trying to comprehend the complexity of achievements: Talent x Effort = Skill, and Skill x Effort = Achievement. What's the common denominator? It may seem like a given that effort is blatantly required to achieve success, but, if so, then why do most people focus on the "talent" a high-level athlete has? I think talent is perceived to be the end-all be-all in sport, and it's something that continues to be debunked in recent research. Talent is simply raw gift and ability. Talent doesn't get you anywhere without effort. Skills can't be refined without effort, either. **Effort** is the predictor of grit, not talent.

Presence

Image courtesy of Pixabay

When I was first interested in mental performance, *Presence* by Amy Cuddy was the first book I read. One thing that I took from Presence is: self-affirmation. Self-affirmation isn't just hyping yourself up, saying, "I'm the best at this" or "I'm never going to lose." Self-affirmation is only effective when it is grounded in the actual truth; it's "reaffirming the parts of our authentic best selves we value most" (Cuddy, 2015). Presence is a number of things. Being present is believing and owning up to your own story, and this is essentially is one of the most important things for mental performance. Presence is also the next five minutes. During times you are the busiest, it's incredibly easy to get lost and distracted by many things. The key is: get into the present moment! When you get into the present moment, you increase your focus, efficiency, and your enjoyment of any task you're set on completing.

Here's a couple of tips on how you can get into the present moment:

1. **Focus on your breath**. Close your eyes. Perform Deep breaths in through your nose and out through your mouth. This pay dividends to calming the mind and body. This allows you to be present within yourself.

2. **Be aware of your surroundings**. Use your senses. Look around you; what do you see? What do you smell? What do you hear? Acknowledging your senses RIGHT NOW, in the current moment, enables your presence.

3. **Talk to yourself**. Talk about the situation you're in at the present moment. Self-talk is incredibly empowering.

4. Do all of the above while also **going for a walk**. As you're on your stroll, be sure to focus on your breath, be aware of what's around you, and talk to yourself (don't look too weird). Discuss the things you need to get done.

Discuss a plan on how you're going to achieve it the moment you get back. Your walk could range anywhere from 5-10 minutes, whatever YOU need. Sometimes it's necessary to go outside, get fresh air, and clear your mind before you can get into the present moment.

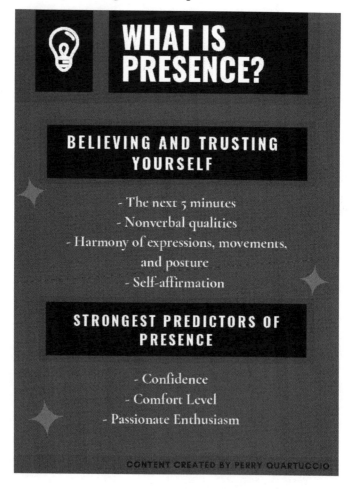

WHAT IS PRESENCE?

BELIEVING AND TRUSTING YOURSELF

- The next 5 minutes
- Nonverbal qualities
- Harmony of expressions, movements, and posture
- Self-affirmation

STRONGEST PREDICTORS OF PRESENCE

- Confidence
- Comfort Level
- Passionate Enthusiasm

CONTENT CREATED BY PERRY QUARTUCCIO

"Belief lifts your talent."

Controllable: Your Confidence

Beliefs lift your talent. This is ultimately the definition of what confidence is. This is something that I took from *Talent Is Never Enough*, a book written by John Maxwell. The biggest obstacle for most people is the lack of belief in themselves. This is an obvious issue because it places an invisible ceiling on your potential. If you do not truly believe you can accomplish something, how do you expect to achieve any goals that you set for yourself? How do you expect to succeed? The first thing you need to do is believe in your potential. The next thing you need to do is believe that you're fully **capable** of fulfilling your potential. Lastly, you must believe your goals are **worth** achieving. This is the time where you self-reflect and figure out why your goal is important to you. If it's not important to you, you won't believe it is possible and you are less likely to achieve it.

Belief ➜ Expectations

Expectations➜ Actions

Actions➜ Results

All of this may seem so simple, but I guarantee you that it's not. When I played, I always had this goal to throw 90 mph. That's every young pitcher's goal, right? To throw 90 mph? As you will read later on about my story, you'll see the things I have learned, what things I have done (drills, training, etc.), and you'll also see that I never achieved that 90-mph goal. I topped out at 81-82 mph. Looking back on my time as a player, I realized

61

that I didn't truly **believe** throwing that hard was **possible** for me. My belief **hindered** my talent.

Controllable: Your Goal-Setting

Goal-setting is crucial for mental performance training. One would think that valuing and hoping for a better future or a better life (components of positive psychology) would allow an athlete to experience a more positive lifestyle and wellbeing, and a better career. However, it seems that when someone values success so much, they have the tendency to set goals that are far from reach. Most people have their own unique definition of what success is and what their goals mean to them. This is fine, however, when goals are not met, a sense of disappointment comes to the individual who set a far-fetched goal. Knowing that a certain goal is never going to be attained sets an athlete back even farther in their career, thus perpetuating a negative outlook on themselves and their ability to reach their potential. H.A Dorfman, author of *The Mental Game of Baseball,* discusses goal-setting in a more in-depth manner. Dorfman implements five points regarding the importance of goals and what athletes must do if they want to achieve them:

1. You must set performance goals. **What** are the goals you want to accomplish? Do you even know what your goals are?

2. You must develop process/action goals. **How** are you going to achieve your performance goals? What are the necessary steps you must take?

3. Goals **direct** and **determine** your behavior. You must create an intentional focus on your goals. Let them drive you. Figure out **why** they are important to you.

4. Goals allow you take risks. Risks are necessary for success!

5. Without goals, your success will float. Without goals, you don't have responsibility or control over your success.

There is this one ongoing lesson that I always remind myself of: we cannot control everything. In baseball, there are a number of things you cannot control: bad calls, freak injuries, etc. Over the last few days, I learned what "Mental Discipline" is, recalling ideas from *The Mental Game of Baseball* yet again. Mental discipline is the ability to control the things we can control (our attitude, preparation, and visualization), as well as finding out ways to respond to the things we cannot control. Mental discipline is also having a goal, knowing what you need to do in order to achieve that goal, and dedicating your time and energy into it.

> **"Fear defeats more people than any other one thing in the world."**
>
> **Ralph Waldo Emerson**

Don't be afraid of failure. Attack your goals head on!

Another thing to consider when it comes to goal-setting: letting go of expectations. Justin Friedman, RHP in the Chicago White Sox Organization and I had an incredible conversation on how expectations get in the way of your success. He also points out that it is imperative to know who you are before they can tell you.

Justin Friedman- Chicago White Sox Organization RHP

Let Go of Expectations

"Once you have decided where you want to go, the rest is irrelevant and incredibly unpredictable. The route you take will undoubtedly be vastly different than anything you could possibly imagine when you initially chose your destination, but the point is that ultimately you will arrive. Letting go of expectations means being willing to adapt the plan as you evolve and learn. It also means that we do not cling to any definite timeline and focus solely on making our vision a reality instead of when it will happen. Regardless of where your journey takes you, the destination remains the same. Plans and timelines that are far too rigid often give people a sense of failure or constantly being "behind" because of some arbitrary schedule they created at their original level of understanding. Not reaching your goal in two years does not mean that you have failed to reach your goal; it simply means that it is going to take more than two years to accomplish. Too many people give up because of a bogus expiration date that they decided to place on their own dreams. And too many others quit because their initial two (or even two hundred) plans did not yield the desired results. Failure is only final if we quit. So, fail often and fail forward, as you walk your unique path to self-actualization and success."

Know Who You Are Before They Can Tell You

"Our sport involves a great deal of evaluation, comparison, and criticism. In order to navigate all of that without losing yourself along the way it is very important to know who you are before people try to give you an identity based on their perceptions of you. While you can and **should** absorb and learn from the input of others, you must not let their opinions of you become your reality. Just because someone sees you a certain way (even if they are an authority on the subject) does not mean that it is how you ought to see yourself. You have probably heard someone say something along the lines of "you've got to block out all the haters." While that statement is true, it is perhaps even more essential to not overvalue compliments either. Praise is the Trojan horse that lets those negative comments sneak past your armor. If you give too much value to validation, you will be equally affected by its opposite because at the end of the day both are rooted in a concern for the opinions of others. That is why I stress the importance of first discovering who you are and what you want, so that you can then engage with the world around you and be receptive to it without internalizing the way it sees you."

Twitter: @jfriedman37 Instagram: @jfriedman37

Controllable: Your Attitude

- We are responsible for our attitude

- Attitude is built by our **thoughts**. Most people live their lives displaying attitudes that are built off of their emotions. Emotions do not and should not direct and control our attitude. Our thoughts do.

- Good attitude= when everyone gives up, you're still believing and hoping. Acknowledge defeat, but you should not be **willing** to be defeated. This is a positive attitude.

- Don't give up!

- Good attitude= being competitive and aggressive. Attack first; don't wait to be attacked.

Controllable: Your Preparation

The athletes who perform the best in the world are the best preparers in the world. Kobe Bryant (may his soul rest in Heaven) is said to have been one of the best preparers in the game of basketball. Kobe's "Mamba Mentality" is something that was instilled in him ever since he was a little boy. Pau Gasol, one of Kobe's teammates and a lifelong friend, had written the foreword in his book, *The Mamba Mentality*. Gasol wrote that one of Bryant's' greatest qualities was his attention to detail—he'd tell his teammates that if they wanted to be really successful, they needed to prepare, prepare, prepare. Preparation is key.

Another example of a high-level athlete praising preparation: Derek Jeter. Jeter wrote in his book, *Jeter Unfiltered*, that his biggest fear in life is to be unprepared. Jeter dwelled on repetition, practice, and discipline his entire career. I even thought his famous "jump throw" was simply something he tried in a game and continued to run with it. I then learned, throughout the book, that he actually developed it in the minor leagues in a practice—just messing around. It wasn't until he practiced it on a day-to-day basis for a while that he then implemented the "jump throw" into a real game.

> **Preparation is another thing we are responsible for; therefore, it is within our control.**

Controllable: Your Mindfulness

Mindfulness is an aspect that is imperative to mental performance training. It's the psychological state in which one is fully aware of the present moment. Athletes, especially those who are in high-level competition, lose sight of the present moment and may undergo a tremendous amount of stress. Gordhamer (2014) suggests, "the benefits of mindfulness practice as applied to sports are almost blindingly obvious. Focus, awareness, clarity of thought, and the ability to stay in the present moment are basic skills for any great athlete." I like to think of mindfulness as a bridge—guiding us to get out of this little box called "reality". This is something that I've found to be very humbling. The ability to take a step back, close my eyes, control my breath, and imagine my physical-self escaping from all of the stress and tension that may be in front of me is exceedingly liberating. This awareness allows athletes to get into the present moment, which will ultimately help them achieve an optimal performance state called "flow" (Glass, Spears, Perskaudas, and Kaufman, 2019). Some examples of "flow" are complete concentration on the task at hand and loss of self-consciousness. Focusing on the task at hand and losing self-consciousness are obviously beneficial for elite performers. These dimensions are highly associated with awareness and acceptance, two main aspects of mindfulness practice (Kaufman, Glass, and Pineau, 2018). When an athlete is faced with adversity, they may find that implementing some sort of mindfulness training gives them that competitive edge over their opponent. The game of baseball, in particular, will do its very best to make sure a player doesn't succeed, but it's up to the player to respond to the curveballs being thrown at them. Mindfulness— being completely aware and accepting of the difficulties in front of them— will certainly assist an athlete in enhancing their performance by increasing their flow, athletic endurance, and ability to balance athletic and personal tasks (Glass et al., 2019).

Controllable: Your Visualization

Another versatile tool in mental performance training is visualization. Visualization enables athletes to imagine themselves in a specific situation. Athletes can get a clear picture of a given situation by using all of their senses in order to better prepare themselves for when the situation occurs to them in real life. This type of training is unbelievably effective. This works for any position player, hitter, or pitcher. For example, a pitcher can place themselves in a situation in which they're visualizing executing a specific pitch—how the ball spins, the location of the pitch, and even the velocity of it. If you experience a scenario vividly in your mind, you will now have the confidence to carry out whatever you imagined because you've already seen it. Imagery techniques can also be performed for skill development, with results showing its effectiveness across a range of skills and abilities (Lindsay, Spittle, & Larkin, 2019). Not only does visualization and imagery practice allow an athlete to gain confidence, it can also result in an increase in sport performance. I believe this can be a game-changer for many baseball players, especially for those who lack confidence in themselves and their ability to succeed.

Controllable: Your Breathing

Here's my $0.02 on breathing techniques/exercises: https://youtu.be/D9tj8SPgqFQ (YouTube Channel

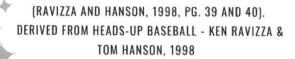

A GOOD BREATH

" 1) GETS YOU IN THE PRESENT MOMENT

2) ENABLES YOU TO "CHECK IN" WITH YOURSELF TO SEE IF YOU'RE IN CONTROL

3) HELPS YOU GET CONTROL

4) HELPS RELEASE NEGATIVES

5) ENERGIZES YOU WHEN YOU'RE FEELING SLUGGISH

6) HELPS YOU SHIFT FROM CONSCIOUS THINKING TO "UNCONSCIOUS" TRUSTING

7) HELPS ESTABLISH A SENSE OF RHYTHM IN YOUR PITCHING, HITTING, OR FIELDING "

(RAVIZZA AND HANSON, 1998, PG. 39 AND 40). DERIVED FROM HEADS-UP BASEBALL - KEN RAVIZZA & TOM HANSON, 1998

CONTENT CREATED BY PERRY QUARTUCCIO

Growth Mindset

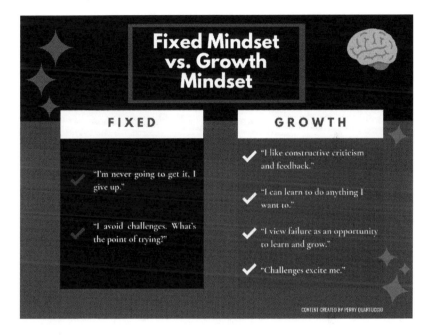

The growth mindset is something that needs to be implemented into all athletes' heads. In Carol Dweck's *Mindset*, she cautions everyone to beware of success. Success makes it very easy to fall into the fixed mindset, where an athlete may believe that they are successful simply because they have "talent". Falling into the fixed mindset, especially in times of achievement, could hinder your full potential as an athlete. Kids who were successful in travel baseball and in high school tend to be bigger than everyone else, more talented than everyone else. Most of the time, these are the guys that miss the boat on the long-term success they can truly achieve. The sheer difficulty and demand of the sport has a potential to catch up to them. They're no longer the big dog in college or in pro ball because every other guy on the team is just as talented as them. This is where you see the downfall of many, many players. On a deeper level, many factors come down to how we think and perceive the things that happen around us. Baseball is a game of failure. The best players in the world are expected to hit .300 or better. That means they fail 7/10 times! The growth mindset praises process— hard work, trying new strategies, and asking for input from others (Dweck, 2016). As I mentioned before (see "Youth Parents"), it's important to not just focus on the accomplishments of the player, but to truly praise the process an athlete took to get to that accomplishment. Implementing the growth mindset is not an easy task, but I firmly believe that if you do get into the growth mindset, you'll have a stronger chance at realizing your full potential and lead a more fulfilling life. You can live a life of enjoyment, learning, and growing.

Mental Toughness

Diving into the research, it seems that mental toughness plays a mediating role between perfectionism and motivation (Cowden, Crust, Jackman, and Duckett, 2019). High-level athletes, (baseball players included) are at risk to undergo mental health issues. Developing mental toughness, defined as a psychological construct linked to achievement in competition, has a profound impact on "adaptive mental health functioning and well-being, lower reported stress and depression, and better sleep quality" (Cowden et al., 2019). This is clearly an appeal to baseball performers. If this is the case, then athletes should put an emphasis on improving their mental toughness, achieving those "7 C's" mentioned in *Mind Gym*.

As simple as this may appear, the literature suggests that this is a much more complicated issue to tackle. Cowden's study indicates that mental toughness is only prevalent when there are true efforts from the athlete to improve their own skill of mental toughness. These efforts also maintain self-determined motivation (SDM). SDM is the type of motivation athletes should strive for; extrinsic motivation or outside motivation will only get you so far. This study found that "creating training environments that mirror high-pressure competitive performance contexts and providing athletes with the necessary psychological skills to deal with such demands" will increase the likelihood of sustaining SDM—So will equipping the athlete with a real understanding of how to deal with adversity and performance-related problems when they arise. I would advise that during practices, players should have an allotted time to perform and compete under intense, difficult, game-like situations. If they rehearse these mental toughness approaches in practice, they'll be able to perform well under pressure when games matter the most.

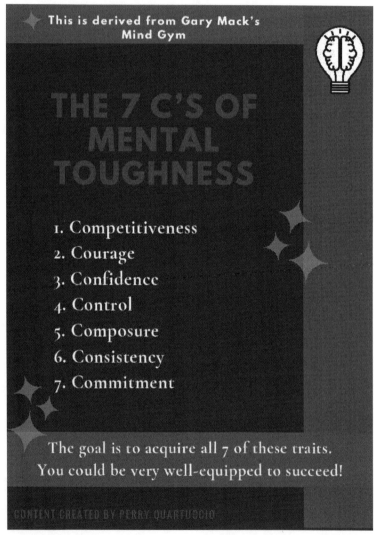

This is derived from Gary Mack's Mind Gym

THE 7 C'S OF MENTAL TOUGHNESS

1. Competitiveness
2. Courage
3. Confidence
4. Control
5. Composure
6. Consistency
7. Commitment

The goal is to acquire all 7 of these traits. You could be very well-equipped to succeed!

CONTENT CREATED BY PERRY QUARTUCCIO

Preparing Players for Life

Mental Performance training has the potential to not only prepare players for just baseball, but to prepare them for life too. This truly resonates well with me. All players know this, even Steve Springer mentioned this too (see page 17) but players love coaches who care for their players. Connecting with players is imperative—being able to reach them on an emotional level is paramount for a player's success and more importantly, their well-being. Mental performance coaches are another resource that players have at can go to for this skill development. John Wooden, arguably one of the best college basketball coaches there ever was, is a perfect example of what it means to be a great coach. Wooden believed that most coaches overcomplicate things. He advised that it's necessary to prepare the player and then just let them play. Wooden didn't only prepare his players with basketball lessons. He prepared them for life, guided each player, and coached them with **concern, compassion**, and **consideration**. That's **why** he was such an amazing coach. Wooden **cared** for his players. Concern, compassion, and consideration.

"Mental training doesn't consist of any gimmicks."

The crazy thing is that mental performance training is what separates the good from the GREAT. Mental training doesn't consist of any gimmicks, though. Many people think it's a simple fix or a basic adjustment. This is something that needs to be developed with consistency and over time. Take time out of your day and hone in on your mental performance skills!

Alan Jaeger- Founder of Jaeger Sports

"Whenever we're asked about the Mental Game, we like to simplify it and make it as easy to understand as possible. We do this by dividing it into two basic components: **Game Management** and **Mental Practice**. Game Management is essentially as it sounds —how can you best "manage" the game, from a strategic approach in order to optimize your performance. Traditionally, you'll hear many common themes such as "Stay in the moment", "Control what you can control" and "Trust the "Process". And though there are many ways to "manage" the game, the essence of our approach focuses on being **process-oriented**, rather than result oriented. From this main "theme", our goal is to get the athlete to understand that by identifying and understanding what their process is, they can then prioritize their focus to a few constants, rather than trying to control countless variables. Clearly, how you approach and manage the game is an essential part of your Mental Game, and thus, it has been given a great deal of attention over the years. But the other component of the Mental Game—Mental Practice, which includes various forms of exercises (i.e. Breathing Exercises, Meditation, Visualization, Guided Imagery) may ultimately have the greatest impact on an athlete, on and off the playing field. Where Game Management can truly help you navigate the game strategically, Mental Practice is just that—a "practice"— something that can be done on a daily basis to help improve " mental skills". These skills include relaxation, clarity, presence, trust, freedom— that not only provide invaluable benefits to a player's mental health and well-being, but can truly help support how an athlete bests "manages" the game with more awareness, effectiveness, and consistency. That's why we place such a great deal of emphasis on the practice; we simply feel that it starts with doing something each day to invest in and nurture your body, mind, and soul. Getting to know yourself on an intimate level, and bringing about this awareness is so essential to the quality of your life."

S&C + Mobility

Photo Credited: Justin Silva

"I'm no expert on strength and conditioning; the guys in this book are."

Strength and conditioning, mobility, and flexibility all kind of go hand-in-hand. They're pieces to the puzzle. It's important to recognize that everyone is built differently. Everybody has different genetics. One thing may work for one person, but may not work for someone else. The key to strength and conditioning training is to find your deficiencies and to exploit them. Recognize them. Embrace them. Work as hard as you can on your weaknesses. Big, stocky guys (like myself) may be excellent in the weight room where moving big weight may be easier for them. A majority of the time, these big guys are incredibly immobile. Their shoulder mobility is poor. Their hip mobility sucks. Long and lanky guys probably don't move that much weight but are probably faster and more flexible. For me, I was a guy who could squat 405+ lbs., deadlift 500+ lbs., but run a 7.3s 60 yd. dash on top of having poor lateral movement and immobile shoulders. I did hot yoga my senior year of high school to increase my range of motion in my hips and more specifically, my shoulders.

I'm no expert on strength and conditioning; the guys in this book are. They're the best of the best. Utilize everything they talk about. Soak up all of the great information like a sponge. As much as the amalgamation of information may be a lot to take in, it's imperative that you find what works best for your body and for your athletic goals.

Video of me Lifting: (YouTube Channel)

Connor Rooney- High Performance Trainer, Driveline Baseball (Pitchers)

"At Driveline, I coach the floor, assess and reassess athletes, program, develop content, and do lots of research for different projects that we may have going on. Before Driveline, I was a graduate assistant at Coastal Carolina. I was supposed to be there for two years, getting my masters and interning with the pitching and strength coach at CCU. After two months, Driveline offered me a position and I couldn't turn it down.

I'd say to never forget the reason why you're training in the first place— that reason being to solely being to get better at pitching. A lot of guys (and I definitely was one of these guys back in college) get caught up with numbers in the weight room or seeing their abs in the mirror. What really matters in the long run is how good you get at throwing baseballs from 60 feet 6 inches. At the end of the day, what you look like in the mirror and how much weight you lift does not matter if you can't get guys out. If you've been doing the same routine for years and you haven't gotten any better on the mound, it's probably time for a new one. Everything you do matters and it's never just as simple as you think."

Instagram: @rooneyperformance

Joseph Potts - Owner of Top Speed Strength & Conditioning.

Head of KC Royals Scout Team S&C

"The best advice I can give to a kid is to do everything in your power to preserve type IIx fiber type function and recognize that success in the weight room does not guarantee success on the field. You can't sacrifice movement ability for the sake of size/strength (in terms of maxes)."

Twitter: @TopSpeedLLC

What are Type IIx fibers?

In short, type IIx muscle fibers are fast-twitch. These muscle fibers provide much more powerful forces than a Type I muscle fiber would. Sprinting, powerlifting, plyometrics, and any other explosive movements are examples of this.

More on Explosiveness...

Nunzio Signore- Strength & Conditioning Coach-Owner of Rockland Peak Performance

Training Power and Explosiveness in the Weight Room

In most sports, we have approximately .150 -.220 ms to produce force to be considered "fast". In many more power-based sports such as baseball or sprinting, this time is even faster.

While strength, or more specifically peak force, is still and always will be the foundation for all other types/speeds of strength to be built upon, the key is to figure out which athletes require more force or, who is better off working at higher velocities and the specific loads needed to produce the training adaptations most specific to their given sport.

As training age increases, these more elite-level athletes will need to focus on applying their newly acquired strength in a more "sport-specific" manner. This involves not only prescribing the appropriate energy systems and training speeds but applying them at the correct time of the year to increase the likelihood of a positive/peak adaptation to coincide with the start of the season. VBT is a training method that evaluates the intensity of a given movement by calculating displacement and time through the monitoring of bar or body speeds. In other words, it is a type of strength training that is based upon the speed of a movement or load lifted rather than the weight of that load based on a percentage of a one-rep maximum (1RM).

The speed output is typically tracked by a piece of technology/ device known as a linear position transducer, which attaches to the bar or more recently wearable accelerometers such as a "Push" band which can be worn around the arm, ankle or waist (center of mass).

These devices help monitor the velocity of a movement, which correlates highly to an athlete's one rep maximum (1RM). Below is a chart I developed based off hundreds of athletes that train or have trained at my facility in the past few years. As you will soon find out, VBT is close but not perfect so it's always best to gather your own database over time. I have shared this one with many coaches who have reaped amazing results.

Velocity (Bar- Body Speed)	Relationship to Est. 1RM
.12-.25	95-100% (est. 1RM)
.25-.50 m/s.	80-95 %
.50-.75	60-80%
.75-1.0	40-60%
1.0-1.3	20-40%

This information provides the coach or the athlete themselves with valuable, external information in terms of the speed/intensity of the lift/movement and can provide instantaneous feedback to the lifter as to whether or not the load is appropriate for the goal of the training session so that load or volume can be adjusted accordingly. More importantly, fluctuations in strength due to stress and fatigue, whether it be from lack of sleep, personal issues or the residual effects of a game or training session the day before can be considered as well.

Average (Mean) Concentric Velocity (MCV)

Average velocity is simply the average speed during the entire concentric phase of the exercise including the time spent decelerating through that range of motion. As strength-based exercises consist of both acceleration and deceleration phases, the mean concentric velocity metric should be used.

Peak Velocity

This is generally programmed in the final 4-8-week block (pre-season). Peak velocity is simply the peak speed during the concentric phase of the exercise and is usually calculating the fastest 5-10 milliseconds of a concentric movement. Ballistic exercises are used where force is produced for a very short amount of time before the implement or body is projected into the air.

The Special Strength Zones

The S.A.I.D. principle stands for the "specific adaptation of imposed demands" and states that training should create the adaptation or trait that is needed to excel in our desired sport. However, what is needed changes from month-to-month and from athlete-to-athlete based on anatomical make-up. One key advantage of training with VBT is the ability for an athlete/coach to ensure that the desired trait they are trying to achieve is being developed. Every type of strength/trait has a speed. If we are not training in the zone of that speed, then we are not developing the strength/trait desired.

This better enables us to monitor an athlete's associated velocities and hone in on the trait the athlete is trying to develop to help improve performance at their specific sport. Training with VBT allows the athlete to pinpoint the specific demands that fall along the force-velocity curve with greater accuracy and in turn better stimulate these adaptations.

1. **Absolute Strength (.25 -.50 m/s)** – This is the range where athletes will see their 1RM fall into, but will not necessarily be where an athlete performs best under heavy load due to the lack of a higher velocity component in the lift.

This strength is generally developed between 1 and 4 reps. The adaptation achieved is increasing the cross-sectional area of the muscle fibers to help create better "stiffness" and increase motor unit recruitment.

Reps- 1-4
Intensity- 80-95% 1RM

https://youtu.be/r3eC6ZpimyM (RPP Baseball)
(Trap Bar D-lift @ 85% 1RM)

2. **Accelerative Strength (.50 - 0.75 m/s)** – Typically an athlete's best force output is done in this strength zone, *especially when load is between 60-65% 1RM.* This is due to the fact that we are still using heavy enough loads to get a strength adaptation, but light enough to allow the athlete to move his body and the bar quick enough to enhance the acceleration side of the force equation (Force = Mass x Acceleration).

Being able to move the bar/body quicker enables athletes to create more peak force than at heavier loads because of the quicker time component used. During the in-season this becomes the trait that diminishes the quickest (7-10 days) and must be maintained.

Reps: 3-8
Intensity: 60-80% 1RM

https://youtu.be/i7MxTE8aVUo (RPP Baseball)
(Trap Bar Deadlift @ 60-80 % 1RM)

3. **Strength-Speed (0.75 – 1.0 m/s)-** This zone sits on and trains the "force side" of power on the curve. This zone's protocol (load) requires near maximum to moderate muscular contractions with a secondary emphasis on the rate of production (velocity).

Exercises Include: Weighted jumps, band assisted/ resisted bench press/dead lifts/squats

Reps: 3-5- or if power output drops by 10 % set-to-set
Intensity: 40-60% 1RM

4. **Speed Strength (1.0 – 1.3 m/s)** – While some athletes sit on the strength side of power (above) others live more on the "velocity" side of power. This zone's protocol is where rate of force production (velocity) takes precedence over force, making (load) secondary in nature.

This is also the velocity where "in-game" movements such as sprinting, cutting and throwing begin to take place.

Speed-Strength is described as "moving a lighter weight as fast as possible"

Exercises Include - weighted jumps lighter loads than used for strength-speed), med ball throws and various forms of plyometrics.

Protocol:

Reps: 3-5- or if power output drops by 10 %
Intensity: 20-40% 1RM

https://youtu.be/dIvZW2Nqd24 (RPP Baseball)

(Trap Bar Jumps @ 20-40% 1RM)

Summary

More recently and in growing numbers, velocity-based training is being used by coaches and practitioners to determine the optimal load- independent of 1RM. It can also be a powerful tool to accurately monitor current stress and/or fatigue on the central nervous system from day-to-day or week-to-week

Alan Trejo- Infielder in the Colorado Rockies Organization

"The determination and mental focus that the weight room has taught me will never go unnoticed."

The best way to separate yourself from other athletes comes down to your performance in the weight room. Every professional baseball player can throw hard, run fast, and hit the ball hard. I am a firm believer that if you can create a faster, stronger, and more explosive version of yourself, the odds will be in your favor. Having a sense of pride on getting stronger will always push you to better yourself as a baseball player. When I began to excel on the sports performance side of baseball, I began to develop more power, my feet got quicker and most importantly my first step on defense got so much faster. I became a better player and added to my tools. However, being in the weight room doesn't always involve throwing weight around. Some days are used to help the body recover and do everything I can to feel ready for that day. I believe a lot of college athletes do not take the time in the gym seriously because it's a HAVE-TO rather than a WANT-TO.

Every time that I step into a weight room, I visualize everything that I must do to get better that day. Once I have a plan of action, I then try my best to execute it to the best of my ability. **I think what a lot of athletes do not do in this setting is visualize**. I relate the failure during training to failure on the field. The result is the same, therefore why not push mentally to do every rep or every swing right to have success? The one thing that I absolutely love about training is that it will check you. It will make you want to quit, puke, curse, or whatever it may be. The same goes with baseball. **The game will humble and suffocate you with failure until you find a way to channel it in a positive light**. This is why I take so much pride in the time I spend at the gym. It can help you excel on the diamond and it also reminds you what it is like to be human and fail.

I think as kids we never stop to think that pushing our bodies through an absurd amount of strain can somehow help us down the road. Without adding strength and size to my build, I don't believe I would be where I am today. The determination and mental focus that the weight room has taught me will never go unnoticed.

So, if you are an aspiring professional baseball player, I think the best course of action you can do is get in that gym and work until you cannot work anymore. Combine that with an unstoppable work ethic on the field and you can put yourself in a great position to be successful.

Tom Kalieta- Strength & Conditioning Coach- Owner of SWEAT Gym

It Starts with a Foundation

When a player is young and still developing, it's important to build a foundation of strength. This allows him to become a better athlete. As the player matures, the movements become more specific to the sport and address his individual needs. A matured athlete acquires good habits and better training techniques, while also showing improved balance, better core strength, and more body awareness. With more body awareness, athletic movements/positions are easier to control.

It Starts with a Warm-Up

The main goal of a warmup is to increase core temperature, improve range of motion, prime the central nervous system, and reduce injury.

Here's a sample warm up I use with my athletes:
Demonstration Video (YouTube Channel)

- ❖ Frankenstein's to jog

- ❖ Knee hug and lunge to jog

- ❖ Hand walk to high knees

- ❖ Lateral lunge to shuffle

- ❖ Backward lunge with a twist to backpedal

- ❖ Single leg toe touches to sprint

- ❖ Walking Quad stretch to high knees

- ❖ Leg swings (forward/back- Side to side)

- ❖ Stride Sprint Glide

- ❖ Explosive Starts

Training the Imbalances

Baseball training is unlike any other sport and how we train for it has to reflect the challenges players face each day and over the course of a long season. On the professional level, games are mostly every day. At the high-school and college level, 4-5 games a week are played. This heavy workload forces players to set up a routine each day, which consists of warming up, stretching, lifting, doing speed/agility work, and other specific player development drills. Take into account the imbalances that develop throughout the season from hitting or fielding from the same side. How these routines evolve can have a major impact on performance in the playoffs or in championship games.

To address these imbalances, it is crucial to incorporate some type of unilateral training into your workout regimen.

This is an example of one of my favorite unilateral workouts—working one side, then the other while usually working the weaker side first. Perform all exercises in order on the one side then complete on the other.

- ❖ Db High Pulls - 5 reps

- ❖ Db Split Squat - 8 reps

- ❖ Db RDL - 6 reps 1-foot broad jump to sprint

- ❖ Db 1-arm Bench - 10 reps

- ❖ Db 1-arm 1-leg Row - 8 reps

- ❖ Db neutral grip curl to press - 10 reps

The Grind

What is it? How to deal with it? Can the grind be to my advantage? Questions like these have puzzled players for years and, to be successful in baseball, each player has to find the answers individually.

The word grind by definition is "hard dull work'" or "boring tedious work". These words aren't very flashy or enticing. How do we convince a kid that he has to "grind" if he wants to become a professional baseball player? How do we tell a kid that he's going to fail many times before he succeeds? Failure is a part of the grind. I believe how a player handles "the grind" can ultimately determine their success or failure in the sport. Training becomes essential in development through each level. Don't be afraid of the grind. Embrace the grind.

HAVE A PLAN, CUSTOMIZE IT, AND BE RELENTLESS. Offseason, preseason, and in-season training are all equally important. Without one, the others are much less effective. After 25 years of training high-level athletes, the hardest workers are always more successful. Everyone's genetic potential is different. This may be true, however, most of us never reach our full potential simply because we don't work hard enough. I often tell the story of a former big leaguer I trained, Ryan Kalish. One random Thursday, he told me that he had to go away for the weekend for a team event. His flight was at 8 a.m. the next day. Ryan then proceeded to say, "If we start by 4 a.m., I can work out, still have enough time to shower, and make my flight." This type of 'hungry' mindset is what makes athletes successful. It's clear that Ryan wanted to accomplish big things; he was hungry and absolutely nothing was going to get in his way. The plan and goals he set for himself were more important than an early flight. How you deal with little things in the offseason will have a major impact on dealing with a slump or worse, an injury in-season.

Instagram: @tksweat

Gerry DeFilippo- Strength & Sports Performance Coach- Owner of Challenger Strength

I am a strength and sports performance coach from Wayne, NJ and I own and operate Challenger Strength, a sports performance facility. I work with athletes primarily of the collegiate and high school levels across multiple sports, but particularly baseball and hockey.

I started my business training athletes at the age of 21 and have been fortunate enough to grow it into something meaningful and successful in a short span of only four years. Over that time, I have worked with 100+ college bound athletes and successfully aided in the paths of 30+ Division I scholarships.

I hope to contribute the rapid amounts of experience I have accumulated in only a short time and the thousands of hours I have spent working with athletes six days per-week for the better part of four years to something practical and useful to readers of this book. My approach is simple when it needs to be, and complex when it has to be, and it has produced some great results I am proud of!

Off-Season Training Tips

When it comes to the off-season, I would say the biggest thing I advise is having a plan!

The off-season is the largest uninterrupted time of training an athlete has in the sense that you can structure it more precisely, have more days of training in light of a lighter game schedule, and can make training more of a priority. With that said, we MUST be able to plan and prepare accordingly.

Here are some steps to do this:

- Set goals (physical, obviously, but also goals related to your sport attributes and how those physical goals can help/correlate).

- Test and assess! (You have to know where you are starting as a baseline, what you need to improve upon, and how your programming should be structured based on testing feedback). Have testing protocol that is reliable and valid.

- Determine how many days you can train to design your initial programming layout.

- Determine what adaptations you need to prioritize (strength, power, speed etc.) and layer them in the base of your program.

- Determine key performance indicators (main exercises) you know you can use as a gauge of improvement.

- Test and assess every several weeks to determine effectiveness of programming and future changes or changes in your programming direction!

Photo Adopted from Pixabay

My basic programming pyramid sheds some light on the overall thought process to building a program!

Also, if I had to make ONE definite suggestion: sprint and jump regularly and definitely at the beginning of your training week!

Programming Pyramid

Build from the bottom-up

- Variations
- Volume, Load, Intensity etc.
- Desired Adaptations
- Metrics/Tests to measure results/effectiveness
- Goals/Needs for Sport (advanced)

In-Season Training Tips

I'm going to keep this simple because it should be VERY simple.

In-season training needs to be flexible and adjustable. You need to account for changes in schedule, fatigue from game play, and much, much more. As such, a schedule that includes most general areas like sprinting, strength training, and plyometrics etc. during a training week are ideal. In-season is too random to allow you the luxury of zoning in on only one attribute like you MIGHT in the off-season.

Additionally, we NEED to continue to push for gains in-season, ESPECIALLY with young athletes. Don't go until the wheels fall off, but don't be afraid to train for results instead of just maintenance.

Lastly, really make use of a good training residuals chart to guide you. Meaning, understand how long certain attributes will last or maintain if left untrained and use that to help you prioritize what you work on. For example, your aerobic conditioning can maintain for thirty days untrained, whereas maximum speed may last for only one week. Keep things like that in mind.

Twitter: @Challenger_ST
Instagram: @challengerstrength

Mobility

Alex Simone, coach and owner of Simone Baseball Performance, is a guy who provided a ton of great content that I used when I played. One thing that is overlooked in baseball: mobility. Check out Alex's page for awesome baseball performance content.

Instagram: @simone_baseball_performance

Full-Mobility Workout #1 (On Alex's Instagram page)

Full Mobility Workout #2 (On Alex's Instagram page)

Active Recovery Workout (On Alex's Instagram page)

Ryan Faer- Performance Coordinator- Cleveland Indians

The Recovery Circuit

One of the challenges of being an athlete in today's internet age is possessing the ability to sift through all of the available information that can be found with a few simple keystrokes and clicks. Today's athlete is anything but under-informed – rather, they are likely to have too much information and too little of a filter to discern what is most relevant to them. For example, most athletes today know the importance of training aspects such as mobility, recovery, and conditioning since that information is so readily available to them. However, whether they have adequate insight into applying that information is another story.

These three topics in particular quite often tend to be misunderstood. There are innumerable methods to tackle each one of these areas. However, in this discussion we will use one particular method of addressing *all three* physical qualities within the same training sessions as a framework to better understand them. And, we will do so in the context of the starting pitcher in baseball.

The role of a starting pitcher in baseball is unique such that the bulk of the stressors placed on both the body and mind take place in a single day, once every 5-7 days. This is "game day" for the starting pitcher: the day in which they can expect to take the mound and throw the greatest number of high intensity pitches in the week, with the most adrenaline coursing through their veins, while under the highest mental stress.

From what we know about pitching a baseball, we can expect the shoulder and elbow to experience a significant amount of muscular damage, as they – along with the entire kinetic chain— undergo tremendous stress from not only accelerating toward home plate with the baseball, but also decelerating the body and arm as well. The high intensity muscular contractions that occur during the delivery cause acute range of motion changes after an outing, and without addressing this, can turn into substantial deficits over time, when stacked up outing after outing.

Under this context, we can appreciate that mobility for a pitcher isn't just about addressing individual limitations, but also the changes that occur (adaptations) as a result of the sport itself. Thus, post-outing recovery should be targeted on regaining acute losses in range of motion, especially at the shoulder and hips.

Another aspect that is important to address in recovery following an outing is Delayed Onset Muscle Soreness (DOMS). Part of developing as a pitcher is practicing at a high level, and optimized recovery allows for better practice between competitions. DOMS, for a pitcher, is predominantly caused by those very same intense muscle contractions mentioned above. As a result of the accrued muscle damage, the muscles accumulate fluids (both good and bad). This inflammation causes the pain we feel with DOMS. Physiology tells us that the removal of this inflammation comes by way of the lymphatic system, which is what we call a *passive system*. To understand this, let's compare it to the circulatory system (heart, arteries, and veins). The circulatory system is an *active system*, meaning the heart pumps the blood throughout this system. The lymphatic system, on the other hand, is passive because the body does not *pump* it actively; instead, we must pump it ourselves by contracting the muscles of the body. This action then pushes these fluids back toward the heart. This is why inactivity following a hard workout tends to cause a lot more soreness compared to active recovery, underscoring the importance of movement through large ranges of motion as a part of the recovery process.

Another important point on the topic of recovery for a starting pitcher: it isn't just about the muscles. We must take into account the nervous system, which includes our brain, brain stem, spinal cord, and nerves. This system not only allows us to handle the mental and emotional stressors of sport and life, but also dictates the effectiveness and efficiency of all of the other systems in our body, *including* the muscles. Optimizing recovery for the nervous system, then, is crucial not only for the sake of itself, but the sake of the body as a whole.

The nervous system is essentially regulated by two systems: the sympathetic and parasympathetic nervous systems. These systems work in opposition of each other, with the former controlling the "fight or flight response", and the latter controlling the "rest and digest response". And, you can think of these two opposing systems as if they are controlled like a dimmer switch that operates the lights in a room: turn the dial one way and the body will focus its efforts on performing and surviving; turn it the other way and the body emphasizes recovery and regeneration. An outing on the mound and all of the stress it imposes physically, mentally, and emotionally turns the dial to 100, so to speak. It is vital that a pitcher works to bring that dial back down to allow for optimized, systemic recovery of the entire body and all of its systems.

One way to inhibit the sympathetic nervous system and encourage the parasympathetic is the use of aerobic conditioning. It is true that slow, steady-state exercise is the opposite of what occurs on the mound (brief, intermittent, high-intensity movements). Much of today's information on the internet points to the potential detrimental effects of long-distance running for pitchers and to the benefits of sprinting. From a bioenergetics standpoint, I do not necessarily disagree with the premise behind these assertions, however I do contend with the vigor of most "expert" opinions on the topic, and here is why:

When training for the needs of the energy system that predominates pitching (the ATP-CP pathway), sprinting does wonders while aerobic training does very little. However, when an athlete is asked to throw hard and often, lift heavy and fast, and sprint at full intensity (not to mention all of the other stressors of life and sport), a dose of aerobic training -- maybe 20-minutes per week -- is not only a drop in the bucket, so to speak, compared to all of their high-intensity work, but it is also conducive to recovering from the anaerobic work, allowing the athlete to come back to train harder again the next day/week.

Now, a final note on the practical application of what we have discussed thus far: as mentioned prior, there are a multitude of training methods and even more exercise combinations to address the recovery and mobility needs of a pitcher. However, one effective means that can tie together everything we have discussed is the *Recovery Circuit.*

The Recovery Circuit is performed the day after an outing, and incorporates 15-30 minutes of continuous exercise at a low intensity (stimulating the aerobic system), intermixing exercises that target the mobility needs of the pitcher (e.g. personal limitations and range of motion lost from the previous outing). Sequencing of exercises isn't necessarily important, as long as the circuit does not become too intense (a heart rate monitor could be used to ensure the athlete stays in the aerobic training zone).

Ultimately, whether the Recovery Circuit is used or not, the principles behind it – including mobility, recovery, and conditioning – are what should drive any training a pitcher undertakes following competition.

Sample Recovery Circuit

20 minutes Continuous…

Lower and Upper exercises designed to bring Heart Rate (HR) up;

Core and Mobility exercises designed to maintain HR;

Soft Tissue Exercises designed to bring HR down

1. **Lower-Body:** Goblet Squat x5

2. **Upper-Body:** Yoga Push-Up x5

3. **Mobility:** Toe-Touch to Deep-Squat Mobility x5

4. **Core:** Deadbug (1-arm, 1-Leg) x5 each limb

5. **Soft Tissue:** Foam Roll Lats x :60 each

6. **Lower-Body:** Cossack Squat x5 each

7. **Upper-Body:** TRX Row x10

8. **Mobility:** 90/90 Hip Switches x5 each

9. **Core:** Glute Bridge March x5 each

10. **Soft Tissue:** Foam Roll Adductors x :60 each

Twitter: @Ryan_faer Instagram: @Ryan_faer

Hitting

**HERE'S A RARE PHOTO OF ME IN THE
BATTERS BOX.**

Sophomore Year (HS)

"I was good at hitting, until I wasn't."

Up until about my junior year of high school, I was a relatively good hitter. I wasn't the "home run hitter", so to speak. I'd define myself as an average line drive hitter. In youth baseball, I was an absolute monster. In high school baseball, I succeeded at the freshman/JV level. I was good at hitting, until I wasn't. Once the game started to speed up, competition was getting better, and velocities were coming at me faster, this was about the moment I gave up the bat.

I have had the privilege to talk to former MLB player Homer Bush and many professional hitting coaches that I wish I had known of when I was developing as a hitter. Most of these guys approach hitting in a way that I have never seen before. I was introduced to this **'Holistic Approach'** to development. Man, I wish I could hit again! If you want to improve your hitting, in any way possible, check out what these guys have to say! You'll learn a ton.

Homer Bush- Former 7 Year MLB Veteran- '98 World Series Champion

"The elite hitters have the most success in the **bottom of the strike zone** first and then the middle of the plate. They have the least success at the top of the zone."

Pitches at the top of the strike zone are complicated.

- It changes the mechanics of our 'regular' swing. We'd be out of groove. We usually practice swinging at the mid-level, somewhat low pitches.

- When you swing at a high pitch, there are adjustments you need to make in that 140-millisecond swing. You're essentially deciding on how to adjust to a high ball in 140 milliseconds.

  o You have to know what that adjustment is.

  o You have to execute that adjustment.

Hitters who have the highest exit velocity DO NOT have the fastest swing path.

- To catch up to the high velocities: You don't need to speed up the hands, you have to move the body better. It's all about body movement.

107

How did you prepare/practice?

- *Player* Homer Bush: short guy- "I was told to just make contact, and run."

  - Practiced: Tee, soft toss, LIVE BP. Worked up the middle and opposite field line drives

- *Coach* Homer Bush (Post-career)- Same preparation... but more emphasis on training the **top** hand

  - Keep the barrel in the zone longer- The top hand controls the barrel!

  - Work on getting the load/stretch. Load= process. Stretch = feeling

  - Keep the top hand facing open as long as possible

Twitter: @BushHomer

Steve Springer- Performance Coach & Major League Scout for Toronto Blue Jays. Former Professional Player for 14 years

The mind is the #1 thing that gets in the way of our performance. How do we become a great competitor in a game of failure? You need to change what you think success is.

If you want be a successful hitter, you need to forget this one thing:

YOUR BATTING AVERAGE

The batting average is the biggest trap in the game. I hit three balls right on the nose at somebody and baseball/softball says I suck. Success is not defined by your batting averages; it is defined by hitting the ball hard. The moment you say, "I don't care what I hit" will be the day your career starts.

My 4 principles of hitting success

1.   Walk up to the plate with confidence.

2.   Have an attainable goal to hit the ball hard.

3.   Attack the inside part of the ball.

4.   Help your team win that day.

You need to be a student of the game. When you're in the dugout, you should be doing one thing and one thing only. You shouldn't be watching the stands or messing around with your teammates. You should be watching the pitcher. Pitchers are creatures of habit. What's his out pitch? What's he throwing in this count?

Is his breaking ball on today? Watch the catcher too—be aware of fakes. If it's 1-0, 2-0, and the pitcher shakes… SIT on that fastball, which brings me up to my next point:

SIT ON PITCHES YOU'RE GOING TO GET, NOT ON PITCHES YOU WANT OR ARE LOOKING FOR.

> Twitter: @qualityatbats Instagram: @qualityatbats

Bill Miller- CSCS

Why Does Exit Velocity Matter For Baseball?

In baseball, batting exit speeds are highly correlative with how fast the athlete can rotate the bat through the hitting zone. Balls will often travel harder when bat speed is higher as long as an efficient collision is made between the barrel of the bat and the ball. "But, hey, what's the difference between a ball hit at 90 and 95 mph? It can't be *that* big of a deal, right?"

Per Baseball Savant, *Hit Probability* increases drastically on balls hit at 95 mph vs those hit at 90 mph. The goal of hitting in baseball is to reach base as frequently as possible, attempting to improve a team's chances of winning by filling the bases up and clearing them with

110

lots of hits and extra base hits. This consistent rise in batting average, slugging percentage, and rate of runs created are seen with each mph of increased exit velocity.

Some numbers to chew on...

Based on 2019 MLB stats	85 mph exit velocity	90 mph exit velocity	96 mph exit velocity	102 mph exit velocity
Batting Average	.202	.246	.333	.579
Slugging Percentage	.206	.256	.382	.763
Home Runs Hit	1	13	119	582

All three metrics that greatly impact a hitter's success are greatly influenced by exit velocity. This makes sense. The harder a ball is hit, the more difficult it is for defenders to make a play on it.

Interesting note: Every batter who accumulated more than 80 at bats in 2018 & 2019 hit at least one ball over 100 mph (yes, even the speedy runners who don't seem to be very powerful hitters). So, if you want to be a hitter at the highest level, it is imperative to have the ability to hit a ball over 100 mph with a wood bat.

IMPROVING EXIT VELOCITY WITH STRENGTH TRAINING

Pressing: The Pec and Anterior Shoulder muscles are shown to have very high levels of activation when swinging, so weaker athletes should focus on improving pressing strength. Research shows that there is a good correlation between bench press strength and exit velocity.

Hip extension: The deadlift and squat and split squat train very forceful hip extension. Part of a reason ground force production transfers into the upper body when swinging is through powerfully extending the hips. Weaker athletes who improve strength in these areas will typically improve their exit velocity.

Upper body pulling: The Lat and Rear Shoulder muscles are highly activated in the lead arm to pull the implement through when swinging. Pull-ups, Lat Pulldowns, Rows and other upper body pulling exercises can improve strength in this area.

Core stability: The muscles of the trunk must fire to stabilize the spine and transfer energy up the kinetic chain. The best exercises for this are anti-rotational chops, Max Tension Planks, Pallof Presses and other maximal effort contraction exercises

It should be noted that the best way to improve and create transfer to the athletic field is through progressive overload. This means that load or reps are added consistently over time to improve overall force production. The goal should be to achieve 5-20 lbs. greater in each exercise every 3-4 weeks.

IMPROVING EXIT VELOCITY WITH EXPLOSIVE MOVEMENTS

Explosive Pressing: Medicine ball chest passes and ballistic pushups help to ensure that the Pecs are producing force at very high speeds.

Slams: Medicine ball slam variations improve explosive capability in the Lats and help produce force at very high speeds.

Plyometrics: Jumps and depth jumps train the lower body to transfer force from the ground explosively into the upper body. Weighted jumps and depth jump variations as well as sprints and repetitive Bounding all do a good job of training for these qualities.

Rotational core power: Rotational medicine ball scoop toss and rotational shotput throw both train force production in a rotational manner. It ensures that the core is functioning properly to transfer force at high speed.

Twitter: @billmills Instagram: @billmillertraining

Trent Otis- Zona Baseball- MLB/MiLB Hitting Instructor

When asked to give my advice to hitters, on any level, I think of that as a loaded question. When dealing with developing my 8-year-old, it's light years away from me working with a Major Leaguer. Not in the sense that I teach the swing differently, but every instructor needs to be cognizant of the hitter they are working with and, in turn, every hitter needs to learn themselves.

At the **youth** level my focus is athleticism, barrel control, and how to create energy transfer into the ball. I don't give many (if any) verbal cues, I use constraints in any drill work. I really want the hitter to learn as much as they can for themselves. I encourage the hitter to experiment, I focus on the setup of the player, making sure they set up in a neutral position not in prototypical "hitting position". I want them to learn how to get into that landing position naturally. Hit the ball hard and hit it far. Challenge them to hit it in different directions with confidence. It's important to praise failure with the proper intent, keep the training environment fun, and remember that it's "us against the constraint" not "me vs. you". I'm not going to pick apart the small details of the swing, but won't ignore video altogether. I use it as motivation— creating fun ways to watch the best hitters and mimic their movements. Most would be very surprised what young hitters can learn by watching and mimicking (see Vlad Jr. swing vs. Vlad Sr swing). Is Vlad Sr. the greatest hitting coach of all time? Or was Vlad Jr. raised in the proper environment with great swing models? Environment is everything with young hitters, create the environment, and let them go! It's their journey. Support them and let them flourish.

When dealing with **middle school/high school hitters**, the initial point still stands; know yourself and be honest! What do you need to get to the next level? Strength, swing mechanics, adjustability/barrel control, etc. are needs hitters may have to address! "See ball, hit ball" in the correct environment could be all the hitter needs, others may just need a weight room. If a hitter has all the strength in the world but zero efficiency and struggles in live games to hit with consistency, he may need some drill work and mechanical changes. The greatest gift we can give hitters is more time—more time to make good decisions comes from being efficient and quick to contact. When great hitters are quick to the back of the zone and concentrate on the path of the bat being in the zone as long as possible, they will have a buffer as far as timing. A large timing window will still lend to in-game production when timing isn't ideal. This is what makes great hitters. If they are early, they can still slug because their barrel is still in the zone. Likewise, if they are a tick late and their focus is 'path at the back of the zone', the ball will still be hit hard and low to the opposite field.

With **professional hitters**, we develop a plan together based on the hitter's needs. Developing quickness and a consistent bat path will lead to more barrels. It's not how hard you can hit one ball, it's how often can you hit the ball hard.

Bat path, quickness, and a large timing window will lead to in-game production. We work through constraint-based drills so the hitter can learn his own movements and his own feels. From these constraints designed for the specific hitter, they develop a routine. Professional hitters don't have the luxury of a down year or two while they are "working on something". They need to produce! The idea is that the daily constraints will, over time, start to leak into the game swings. Routines can be adjusted to fit current needs or to address specific pitchers, but when in competition, a hitter should not be "thinking" about his swing. They're trying to get good pitches to hit and get off a swing as often as possible. Trust the constraints: the routine will lead to long term learning and consistency.

Why do I use constraints so often?

The best training doesn't come from jogging a memory, it comes from creating a new one.

Ever messed up bad at your job? Making a meal maybe? You won't forget that, that's what we want our body to feel in the swing. Not a swing *thought* that works today and is gone tomorrow.

We want to create a swing memory!

Drop drill for swing quickness: Get into your stride foot down, launch position and learn to move fast. If you shift to swing the body will move and the ball will hit the ground.

Large timing window and a good bat path will allow a hitter to hit all four of these balls and every ball inside of this box hard. The hitter's goal is to create energy through centerfield, no matter what pitch location. Timing of contact will determine where the ball goes on the field. Hit it out front (red arrows), the ball will go to the pull side. Hit it deeper (yellow arrows), the ball will go to the middle/opposite field.

Two tee – high tee. Constraint for the feeling of staying above the ball, with a flat path.

117

Use the net as a wall constraint to keep the energy toward CF.

Twitter: @Zona_Baseball

Jordan Stouffer- MiLB Hitting Coach- Cincinnati Reds

Two Strike Hitting

We spend roughly half of our game at-bats in two strike counts, but I rarely come
across someone who feels comfortable or has a plan with two strikes. We want to
think of every at-bat as at least three opportunities to execute hard barrel contact.

The count is irrelevant in terms of what our intent is, which is to inflict damage on
the baseball. To me, the count only dictates how much of the "strike zone" I am

covering and what I might be able to anticipate in terms of pitch type. Overall, my intent and swing stay the same.

Here are a couple things I want to cover with two strike hitting:
-   What pitchers are trying to do with two strikes.

-   How much is anxiety and fear of striking out putting a shadow on my true ability?

-   What adjustments are effective and what adjustments I recommend avoiding.

-   How timing and posture affect decision making and vision

What pitchers think with two strikes:
As hitters, we forget that a pitcher feels a similar anxiety to produce results.

Having an idea of what pitchers are doing, thinking, and processing in each two-strike count might help. The equivalent of a coach being mad about us striking out looking is the feeling a pitcher gets when he makes a bad two-strike pitch that gets hammered.

0-2 ➜ an off-speed in the dirt, elevate FB, nastiest slider, chase pitch, use the edges, expand the zone, don't leave one over the heart of the plate

1-2 ➜ a best pitch for a strike, use the edges, execute pitch in hitters' cold zone, finish the job

2-2 ➜ a more anxiety, one pitch to work with, FB location has to be perfect, off-speed needs to be thrown with conviction

3-2 ➜ a result is going to happen, best pitch for a strike (higher likelihood of FB), anxiety is high and possibility of trying to be too perfect works to hitters' advantage, good pitcher is confident to execute any pitch for a strike here

How much is anxiety and fear of striking out putting a shadow on my true ability?

Every hitter's worst fear is the fear of striking out and, more specifically, striking out looking. If you've broken free of this fear, you have found greener pastures! There are a lot of factors that contribute to why this causes fear—coaches, parents, offensive philosophy, pressure from teammates, etc. What we need to remember is that we chase and lose our approach when we obsess about the possibility of striking out or have a misled desire to ensure we get a hit to keep our batting average from dropping. It seems that after the first pitch of the at-bat, that anxiety can begin to creep in. We begin to chase pitches and deviate from our approach in an effort to "get our hit" or "put the ball in play." Understanding your "hot zone" is a whole other discussion, but I would rather my hitters give me their best effort with their best swing on a two-strike pitch than to dissolve their swing into a less-competitive one. We want to be the best version of ourselves in all counts. If we are changing our swing to manipulate the barrel unnaturally, shrinking ourselves, tensing up, and becoming less athletic overall, we can expect that roughly half of our at-bats are not our best effort. How are we going to put up the long-term numbers we want? How are we going to help our team if we are actually a less competitive hitter with two strikes?

Effective adjustments vs. ones I recommend avoiding

Effective adjustments with 2k:
- ➤ Physical adjustments:

  - o Choke up

    - ▪ Creates a shorter lever without changing the swing. Might even provide a placebo effect.

- ➤ Box position

  - o Allows you to cover a pitch location or speed that you anticipate.

- ➤ Expand your timeline

  - o Start earlier and give yourself more time to make decisions without the possibility of being rushed.

Mental or approach adjustments:
- ➤ Split the plate vertically or horizontally

  - o Anticipate a side of the plate the pitcher has a tendency of pitching to.

- ➤ Change your target

- ➤ Trust

- o Have a routine that allows you to reset and calm down.

- o Trust yourself and your plan- it still won't work out every time but have the fortitude to think "big picture."

➤ On-time for FB

- o FB is what we want to hit so don't be late.

- o If you get off-speed, you should be able to pull it and continue your swing.

Adjustments to avoid:

➤ Excessive posture and positioning changes

- o As a pitcher, I become more confident seeing a guy become a smaller, less powerful version of themselves.

➤ Focusing on ground balls

- o Ground balls don't translate to hits and sometimes cost us two outs (double play).

➤ Starting the swing later

- o Causes rushing

- o Causes us to be late to fastballs

➤ Taking away rhythm or normal timing mechanism

- We don't practice that type of swing very often so why would be use it when we are fighting our toughest battles

➤ Focusing on the foul line as a target

- Keep your focus on the heart of the field

How timing and posture affects decision-making and vision:

My ultimate indicator of hitting success is making good decisions and being on-time as often as possible. When we control the strike zone and are on-time, we don't have to be as perfect with our movements and mechanics. If you are a great mover AND on-time, your ceiling will be very high in the game of baseball. When I feel rushed, I chase bad pitches and perceive hittable pitches more poorly than I would if I had given myself a better timeline.

To be clear, the word "timeline" is how I describe the time it takes from
swing start (beginning of my first move to load) to contact.
Rushing puts me in bad positions and forces more compensations to get to
the baseball. On the other hand, a swing that is started with enough time to get
energy going will allow my brain and body to focus on the perception aspect
(seeing and recognizing the pitch). My head is more still, my best energy to hit the

ball hard is present, and my highest likelihood to make a late, athletic adjustment
is available when I am on-time.

Twitter: @Hittingforpower Instagram: @hittingforpower

Trey Hannam- MiLB Hitting Coach- New York Mets

Building a Complete Hitter

"Exit velocity is useless if you cannot cover multiple pitches with multiple depths and drive the ball to multiple fields." - Craig Wallenbrock

As I begin to work with a hitter, I start reverse engineering their personal process on how they became who they are. The hitter's individual breakdown of themself personally in detail helps us have a clear understanding of what's happening mentally and physically.

Context is something that not many talk about when working with hitters. Being able to understand what they're trying to achieve, how and when they're going to achieve it, what other coaches are advising them to do, how their body feels, and what level are they playing against, and what their end-goal is are all factors that I need to consider. Once we break all that down, we start to put the pieces back together on how we plan on working together to put the puzzle together in a time efficient manner.

How do we create the best hitters?

1. **Vision** - This has to be the absolute #1 for hitters, logically. You cannot aim well or be on time with what you cannot see well. You have to ensure that the body movements being created don't impede the ability to see the pitch as clear as possible.

2. **Building Trust in Your Work** - Trust the work being put in. Know that you're consistently putting yourself in a great position to do damage vs. multiple types of pitches. Know that you're in a position to hit his best fastball, as well as being able to control yourself for an off-speed pitch due to the training. Your timing doesn't need to be perfect on

every swing—lessen the pressure on yourself not needing to be perfect while being capable to drive a ball at any time.

3. **Timing** - Build an understanding with the hitter on what helps them move when they want to: reacting on the incoming pitch. Educate them with a mirror, video, and feel, so that athletes can control themself against situations where they cannot control anything in competition. Let's be honest, sometimes they cannot even control the strike zone(s).

4. **Movement efficiency** - This is always a controversial subject. I don't talk publicly about it much. To keep it simple, understanding how the hitter moves is very important. Tight mover (Trout, Judge) vs. Loose Mover (Betts, Harper). An example would be to imagine Trout's body as a rubber band. He would be the short, tight rubber band that has less to do to shoot. Betts would be the long, skinnier band that has to be stretched back further in order to release its full strength. Understanding how they move helps you comprehend how you cannot create the least amount of "slack in the rope" for them to react when the ball tells them to "snap" or launch. From there, we look at putting them in an athletic

and balanced position to pull their move TO and THROUGH the hitting zone fluidly. I'm huge on "distance = time" in your swing. You must lessen the distance needed to square up the inside of the desired contact point in order to have the ability to see the pitch longer and make later adjustments when desired. A major thought process that I tell hitters: "You're swinging the whole way until the ball tells you not to. Think and swing back through the pitch without making a jerky, 'start-stop' movement that may hinder your vision or direction. Flow through the ball!"

Types of training environments I create for hitters? Depends on the situation, types of hitters, where they are in their development (**Yes, MLB or MiLB hitters are still in development**)

I ensure hitters in my groups or training are constantly focused on the task at hand. Then, I lighten the mood to compete for some time to make sure they don't overthink situations. Let your training and confidence take over to win every drill or pitch! Target games, drills vs. controlled machine, barrel counts, and staying focused on the plan without getting lackadaisical about it are all crucial. I am a huge advocate of drill work 90% of training, ingraining certain types of movement and constraints, while still focusing on barreled-up balls into the outfield. Don't take swings to just swing; drill yourself to hammer in efficient movement patterns to get the job done.

Twitter: @tjhannam10 Instagram: @tjhannam10

Donegal Fergus- MiLB Hitting Coordinator-Minnesota Twins

What do you work on with hitters on the professional level?

We focus on all aspects of their offensive game. We are trying to develop big league hitters, so, daily work on their mechanics, their mental process, their visual-neural responses, and their competitive testing of these skills are included. With mechanics, we focus on balance, connection, sequence, and body awareness. In our mental process work, we try to give our players confidence in their preparation through a wide array of tactics, such as breathing, visualization and approach planning (See "Mental Performance"). We also facilitate vision training methods such as occlusion exercises, strike zone awareness, and pitch recognition guidance.

Are there any specific drills you can share that are a staple in what you do with your hitters?

We focus on creating a training environment that allows players to explore their own strengths and weaknesses so we work less on specific drills. We do, however, have a few staples we encourage our guys to utilize. The first one is Saddle Series. Player starts with his feet open to the pitcher at a roughly 45-degree angle. With flexion in the legs, the player coils into what would be a prime load position. The player should feel a swing window to the elevated pull side open up by virtue of his foot placement. Start with front toss and progress to slow breaking ball machine. This drill encourages the player to connect with the ground and create both force and swing initiation from the feet up. It also encourages proper barrel angle and swing path on the pull side. Players describe feeling like they have more room to work the barrel out front to a proper contact point.

Another drill series we use with our players is variable machine work. Either with one or multiple machines, adjust the height or angle every few pitches (even turning on and off quickly to slow wheels down) during a round. This engages players' brains and forces them to focus on proper visual awareness.

Minor leaguers are already great hitters, clearly, but what distinguishes them from HS/college hitters?

The single biggest separator between pro hitters from everyone else is their ability to take their high-end swings more often. Consistency of accessing their more optimal swings is what they do better than the rest. From a technique standpoint, they often have the same or only marginally better mechanics than college players, but they take fewer panic or sloppy swings. The *obsession* with daily preparation and development is another separating factor for professional players. The internal drive to be great at their craft consumes the vast bulk of them and keeps them in search of answers.

Lastly, what is one piece of advice you can give to younger hitters to develop their game and make it to the next level, whether that be collegiately or professionally?

Don't be afraid. Don't be afraid of anything. Seek answers and solutions to your problems. Take ownership of your own development and work tirelessly to improve your skills. Your mechanics are a huge piece of that puzzle, but your mindset and the way you approach standing in the box and competing is an even bigger one.

Twitter: @coachferg Instagram: @donegalfergus

Jarret DeHart- Assistant Hitting Coach- Seattle Mariners

Hitting as a Complex Problem

As coaches, we all have a tendency to view player development through a reductionist lens. We are naturally inclined to over emphasize areas of performance that are specific to our domain. When a player is not meeting an expected standard of performance, typically, each coach that touches the player has a different take on the underlying mechanism; the strength coach and athletic trainer point to movement limitations, the sport psychologist points to poor mental skills, and the hitting coach sees technical inefficiencies.

Identifying first cause is futile, as these domains are codependent and interrelated. Movement limitations must be considered in the context of the athlete's technique and in-game movement solutions. Technique can only be assessed with an understanding of the athlete's movement capabilities, in addition to their perceptions and cognitions; the psychological and physical aspects of skill execution are indivisible. Therefore, optimizing player development requires an integration of the physiological, psychological, technical, and tactical aspects of performance. If we fail to integrate information from these domains, it is likely that in designing a development plan for a given player, we will end up "digging in the wrong direction". The hitting coach may try to cue the player into a movement solution that they are physically incapable of attaining. The strength and conditioning coach may attempt to address a movement limitation that the athlete has built robust compensations around; theoretically, by improving this limitation, the athlete's technique could be negatively affected. The need for a holistic model of player development is clear, as we cannot understand any single aspect of performance without the context that the other domains provide.

The question then becomes: how do we determine which aspects of performance should be addressed for each individual? The goal is always to optimize in-game performance; therefore, our holistic model must work backwards from the game to both address the hitter's limiting factors and maximize his or her dominant qualities. By doing so, we can avoid some of the pitfalls mentioned earlier, ensuring that the development plan has a direct connection to the athlete's in-game performance goals. Even if we work backwards from the game to view the hitter through a holistic lens, we will still make mistakes. Developing hitters will always be a challenge, and this is what makes coaching and player development a worthwhile endeavor. With that being said, it is important to remember the famous aphorism in statistics, "all models are wrong, but some are useful". A holistic model that works backwards from the game gives us the best chance to develop a plan that meets the needs of each individual. By viewing hitting as a complex problem, we can avoid the dangerous pitfalls of reductionist coaching.

Twitter: @JD_Hitting

More on the Holistic Approach to Player Development Culture...

Brian Pozos- Hitting Coach/Private Instructor

Individualizing the Development Process

Generalized vs. Individualized Approach: "Avoiding Confirmation Bias"

- When we watch MLB hitters in slow motion video, it becomes easy to see what we intend to see in the swing. The problem with slow motion video analysis is that we are rarely accounting for what we do not see, which is each hitter's day to day practice routine. Each hitter has a history of movement practice that helps shape what we see during their game performance. In order to better understand the individuality that exists from player to player, we must analyze hitters and pay attention to similarities and differences that exist between them.

- When we pay adequate attention to how each hitter is different, we take better care to avoid the confirmation bias that comes with slow-motion swing analysis. It is easy for each of us to pay attention to what agrees with our preconceptions, but it is even easier for us to ignore what fails to agree with our perspectives. These anomalies or inconsistencies can provide us with incredible information and insight, because they encourage us to broaden our perspective, and challenges us to further explore what we currently believe to be true.

- A generalized approach seeks to find the similarities among hitters and provide a clear-cut path to "what all hitters must do". Though this approach can be helpful in understanding the swing, it limits our ability to help hitters, because it limits the many ways each individual might view their process of development. An individualized approach is the job of each coach, because it pays greater attention to the unique characteristics, personalities, and movement capabilities of each athlete. When it comes to working with any athlete, the only consistency that we can depend on is that everything is individually-based.

Reduction & Synthesis: Existence is Relationship

- The reductionist approach has good intentions because it breaks down an idea into digestible pieces. Think of this approach in the context of children, and why they tend to break toys apart. They are seeking to understand how the toy works by breaking it into its pieces and studying each part. The child doesn't truly understand the inner workings of that toy until he or she is able to successfully put that toy back together. This is the balance that synthesis provides for a learning process. The learning process is deeper when an individual learns to understand the pieces and how they work together to make the whole.

- My bias is that all things exist only in relation to other things, and we must constantly seek to understand how all information only holds meaning in context. An example of this can be taken from Alan Watt's example that the word "bark" can have different meanings, depending on how we use it in a sentence. The dog's bark is very different from the bark of a tree. When we apply this to hitting principles, we can begin to understand how different parts of the development process exist in relationship to one another. The hitter's batting stance will influence how the hitter moves to hit the ball, and this move will influence how the hitter proceeds to swing the bat.

- In the macro perspective, the movements that an athlete reinforces in the weight room will have an effect on how the athlete moves in the box. How a hitter practices in the training environment will greatly influence the way that athlete performs in the game environment. How that hitter performs in the game will likely influence how that athlete continues to practice in the training environment. Beyond physical factors that exist in the hitter's environment, the psychological and emotional development of that athlete will also greatly influence the way that athlete perceives failure and success during play.

Perception, Action, and Intention

- The most important factors within the player development process are guided by how the hitter perceives a given task. This perception or understanding will guide the hitter's intentions; perception will influence what the hitter tries to do and why. This is the reciprocal relationship that exists between our perceptions and actions. They cannot be separated, because perception and action are two ideas that are married to one another. An example of this can be easily demonstrated by asking multiple athletes to perform the same movement. Each athlete will express and perform this movement uniquely due to the way each of them understand the task.

- A coach's role is to understand the individual's perceptions about hitting, in order to provide adequate guidance to their development. Rather than trying to direct movements alone, we can attempt to change their perceptions about movement in order to influence their actions. This limits the amount of "cookie-cutting" we employ in our coaching approach. If we pay great attention to the intentions of each athlete, we become better equipped to guide both their perceptions and actions.

Attention, Information, and Emotion

- In the practice environment, we have the most amount of opportunities to direct each hitter's attention. Each hitter focuses their attention on different information that exists in the environment. For example, one hitter might focus directly on ball flight, while another pays more attention to how their body is moving. If we assess where each hitter pays the most attention, we can provide them with better information to direct their attention, which will be different for each hitter. For younger athletes, there tends to be lower levels of body awareness that many understand to be "natural athleticism". If we do a good job with developing their awareness for their movements, we can preserve athleticism and limit rigid and robotic movements.

- Information is plentiful in the training environment, and if overloaded with too much information, a hitter can overthink their swing process. We want to limit the amount of "thinking" they do, and try to encourage more focus and concentration on the task, so they can be creative and natural in their learning and problem-solving process. The more they begin to view their actions, intentions, and results simply as information, they can begin to limit how emotion can affect their performance. Specifically, within baseball, we want our hitters to be able to see each swing as additional information, rather than as "good or bad". If they focus on accomplishing tasks, they can focus less on "fixing" a flaw, or trying to repeat a "good" swing.

- I stole this idea from Chris Colabello at one of his talks at ABCA as he explained that every single swing is attached to an emotional reaction. This is an inevitable part of training, because a hitter obviously wants to improve and problem solve accordingly. The problem that emotions can play is that frustration from past results can interfere with their ability to focus on the task. On the other hand, happiness with what they perceive to be a "good result" can also shift their attention away from the task at hand, and bring their focus to repeating a swing. The problem with this is that each swing is unique, just as each pitch is unique. Within baseball, it is extremely important to learn how to focus and play pitch to pitch.

Solutions only exist in relation to highly specific and complex problems

- The idea that solutions can be generalized is quite silly to me because each problem is not only unique in itself, but each individual perceives the problem differently. The way an individual interacts with a problem, combined with the movement capabilities of that hitter, will tell us what solutions might exist for him or her. Problems are rarely uni-dimensional, and can often be approached from a variety of different angles. Maybe a swing problem is not entirely mechanical, maybe that problem is rooted in perceptual or emotional aspects. Just like the development process, the problem-solving process will be different for every athlete.

- Finding the right solution can begin with first identifying the right problem. Oftentimes we can lead a hitter astray if we are focusing on trying to fix the wrong problem. I stole this from Richard Feynman, but he explains that oftentimes the amateur is only capable of recognizing features of a given problem. In comparison, the expert has a better understanding of the deeper principles of the same problem. If we are seeking to improve upon features of the problem, we might be paying too much attention to symptoms of the problem rather than the root of the problem. Maybe sometimes the problem isn't rooted in one aspect, but in a combination of multiple determining factors.

- The development process is complex, dynamic, and nonlinear. We as coaches will fail far more than we will succeed, and unfortunately the same goes for our athletes. The most we can do is try to fail better and limit how much we fail. In order to find true solutions for our hitters, we cannot always solve problems for them, but help them understand how to solve problems on their own. At the end of the day we want to help mold self-sufficient hitters, because the reality is, we will not be the last coach to work with them. They are going to be exposed to a number of coaches, and a plethora of information. If we are truly trying to help them in baseball and in life, they must be able to learn how to be independent, and search introspectively in order to solve problems and further their own development. We as coaches play a small, but important role in helping them become better athletes, and more importantly, better people.

Twitter: @brian_pozos

Jason Stein- Assistant Coach/Hitting Coach- Duke University

"The best hitters hit. They hit all the time and they spend most of their time hitting things that are extremely difficult to have success against (i.e. pitching machines, live pitching, BP arm that tries to get them out, etc.) Our sport is the only sport where our training environment does not match what we are seeing in particular, facing live arms."

Pitching

Height Doesn't Measure Heart

I was a pitcher for as long as I could remember. I grew up idolizing Roy Halladay and Mariano Rivera. It was not until my freshman year of high school that I developed my obsession for pitching. I also grew fond of watching Marcus Stroman compete. I stood (still stand) at 5'7 and had the biggest aspiration to commit to a Division 1 college, make my way through professional ball, and get called up to the big leagues. I've always had this vague dream of making it to the MLB, but Stroman unlocked the clear vision of my dream at age 14. Marcus is also a short guy, topping out at 5'8. He dominated at Duke and had an impressive 11-6 record his rookie year in 2014. Stroman also pitched well with the Blue Jays, bounced back from an ACL injury, and plays the game with a ton of energy. I wanted to "Be Like Stro".

HDMH. "Height doesn't measure heart." -Marcus Stroman

Those four words stuck with me my entire high school career and still do to this day. I was ready to work as hard as I could to be the best pitcher I could be.

I didn't throw that hard, I've only ever topped at maybe 81-82 mph my entire life. Chasing velocity was always the goal of mine. Chasing that 90 mph. mark. I tried everything you could think of. I had Lantz Wheeler's core velocity belt and Driveline's weighted baseballs and plyo balls. I even incorporated Brent Pourciau's Top Velocity medicine ball drills into my training regimen. I would long toss, do bands, and lift heavy weights. I did towel drills, a ton of mechanical work, and even went to a velocity boot camp. You name it, I did it. I never threw 85 mph in my life. This was self-defeating, no doubt. In the end, it seems as if I trained as hard as I could for two years just to throw 82 mph. It turns out that velocity isn't the end game; there's no cookie-cutter aspect that shapes pitchers' successes.

The point is this: I had all of the tools. I had a pretty good understanding of what it took to throw hard and what I needed to do. Even with all of the fancy tools and all of the overwhelming knowledge, I had not figured it out. Why? I wasn't **consistent**. Consistency is the name of the game— repetition, repetition, repetition. It's not just performing "dry reps" either. In order to become a better pitcher, you must execute countless amounts of consistent, good, and beneficial reps over a long period of time. It's better to do a little a lot, than do a lot a little. I did a lot, a little. I didn't succeed because I wasn't truly measuring what worked for me and what didn't. My mental game sucked. My consistency sucked. You could have all of the knowledge, technology, and tools in the world, but if you don't know how to apply that knowledge, know what works for you, and repeat it as much as you can over a long duration of time, you're not doing yourself any good.

I have had many conversations with the people who have contributed to this section. They all seem to agree with the idea that there's no cookie-cutter way of going about anything. I assembled the best guys to talk about specific topics ranging from arm care, long toss, velocity development, command, pre/post game routines, and pitch design.

Alan Jaeger- Founder of Jaeger Sports

"Take care of your arm so it can take care of you."

ON Our Arm Care/Throwing Programs

Our Throwing Program can be broken down into 2 Major Components: Arm Care and Throwing (Long Toss). Though there are countless ways to prepare an arm for throwing, the main point here is to have a plan that ensures that your arm is extremely warmed up and prepared prior to picking up a ball. Thus, our program specifically focuses on a very in-depth Arm Care Routine involving two major steps: **Arm Circles** and **Band Work**. Arm Circles provide a great deal of range of motion, blood flow, small muscle attention/balance and prepare the arm for step two, or our J-Band Program (which feature 11 Exercises). Again, there are many options when it comes to Arm Care and Arm

146

Prep, but we have found that Band Work/Resistance Training prior to the athletes throwing is simply one of the most efficient, effective and optimal ways of prepping the arm prior to the act of throwing. Once the athlete has finished their Arm Care Program, they are ready to throw. Throwing isn't simply about going out and playing catch without a plan. There are many important principles to keep in mind when going through your throwing routine. The main principle we teach is to "Listen To Your Arm" — only you know on any given day (based on what kind of shape your arm is in) how many throws to make, how far to throw and whether or not your arm is ready for high intent throwing, or what we call "Pull-Downs". Our Throwing Program (Long Toss Throwing Program) is based on two major principles: The **Stretching Out Phase** and the **Pull-Down Phase**. The Stretching Out Phase is designed to position the arm to do just that...stretch out. The idea is that an athlete doesn't want to do anything with high intent unless that particular muscle group is completely "opened up" (stretched out), and thus prepared to handle it. Thus, the Pull-Down Phase doesn't even come into play until an athlete has first fully stretched their arms, which could take anywhere from 3-4 weeks, depending upon the amount of days that athlete is throwing. Assuming an athlete is in great shape, and their arm has been fully stretched out, they are then ready for the second phase of our program, or the Pull Down Phase, which is essentially, taking your furthest throw that day (i.e. 300 feet), and maintaining the intent of that throw, without decelerating as you make your way back in to your partner until you get no closer than 70 feet (for safety reasons). At the end of the day, it's about taking CARE of your Arm so your arm can take CARE of you. Yes, it may take some extra work to invest into an Arm Care Program, but how important is the health, strength, conditioning and longevity of your arm to you?

Twitter: @jaegersports Instagram: @jaegersports

Here's a photo and some clips I took of Dodgers' own Clayton Kershaw performing his Jaeger Band routine.

Kershaw's Routine on an off-day (YouTube Channel)

THE IMPORTANCE OF HIGH-LEVEL ROUTINES FOR PITCHERS ARE DISCUSSED.
(pages 149-160)

Jono Armold- MiLB Pitching Coordinator- Texas Rangers

There are a multitude of factors that differentiate true *professional* athletes from amateurs, all largely dealing with talent, skill, and ultimately performance. Undoubtedly, top-end professional pitchers have incredible pitch repertoires in addition to the skills of command and feel that have been honed over years of hard work and determination. An often overlooked facet of the gap between professionals and amateurs exists in the level of preparation professional athletes must adhere to just in order to survive professional baseball, let alone to thrive. The gap in skill and talent at the upper levels of the game is incredibly narrow. A professional athlete is not merely defined by the ability to perform at 7 o'clock, rather the performance at 7 o'clock is often dictated by the time, effort, and preparation put in during the minutes, hours, days, and weeks spent leading up to that 7 o'clock game. This section of the eBook is designed to be a relatively broad overview and generic covering of why preparation is important and how you can make it work for you. The hope is to create an understanding that there is a certain level of mental and physical preparation required to perform at the highest of levels and what that sort of preparation looks like. In the interest of brevity and for the purposes herein, we will not step into the weeds of specific activities (such as exact arm care exercises or throwing program routines), which will undoubtedly be covered in other sections by other experts.

One of the most basic components of preparation involves having a *routine*. In its definition, routine means structured, repeated, and objective, however a *true routine* can be fluid, adjustable, and subjective. We must first understand that a routine is only as good as its ability to aid your performance. A routine is designed to *help you*, not to *hurt you*. This is a concept that many athletes struggle with, especially when a routine becomes ritualistic and inflexible.

The greatness of a routine is rooted in its simplicity of application; having a beneficial routine takes neither skill nor talent. It takes no massive effort or brainpower. It is something that should be yours and something that helps you to be and feel prepared, not something that constrains or confines you. Merely having a routine will not improve your stuff but it will improve your ability to be consistent in your work and performance, thereby assisting in your ability to "be where your feet are" while simultaneously maintaining a long-term vision. It takes discipline and a narrow focus but can also loosen the potential vice of anxiety and overthinking that can often surround competition.

A routine is merely a means to an end and for one to be effective, there must be high clarity of what the immediate mission is. The thought cannot be, "I can only do XYZ because it is my routine." Rather, the question must be asked, "Am I making progress with this routine, or do I need to alter XYZ to get the results that I want my routine to achieve?" Heavily involved in this holistic process is also the need for perspective in order to truly plan your work. What are your most immediate needs in order to develop your most pressing skills? As an example, if I am currently in-season and the primary goal of my routine is to be at my strongest on gameday, my plan and routine needs to embody that goal. Long tossing the day before my game may not achieve my desired result. I may have to minimize my pitches in the bullpen that I typically throw two days before the game. Am I properly hydrated and what pre-game carbohydrates put me in the best possible position to have success when I need it most? On the contrary, if my goal is to improve pitches in practice, then my routine should be more focused on the mid-week bullpen and throwing program during the days in-between competitive outings. Keeping these things in mind, a routine is basically having a plan— a plan for the day with your own end-goal in mind. Greatness lies in the discipline that comes from the commitment to and execution of that plan.

Regardless of your own personal and developmental goals, it is important for you to learn, develop, and take ownership of *YOUR* daily routine. It should be highly individual and *should* vary from person-to-person. This includes a detail-oriented understanding of your throwing; from potential weighted ball work, to a throwing program, to bullpen sessions, both during the week and prior to a competitive outing. However, a proper routine extends outside of just throwing and into *all* of the things that *enhance* your throwing. In professional baseball, your routine will be heavily influenced by multiple departments including the strength and conditioning department, the athletic training department, the nutrition department, and the player development department as well as others. Where in one area you may be strong, other areas can provide the 'lowest hanging fruit' for both your immediate and long-term development. In many ways, this makes the game like a race without a finish line because there can always be improvement and refinement.

It is mentioned earlier that a routine is designed to *help you*, not to *hurt you*. On its face, this concept seems rather rudimentary and self-explanatory, but, regarding your personal preparation and the routine therein, you must ascertain if there is enough flexibility and adjustability for it to be sustainable. Can you do your routine or a version of it in a rain delay? What if the field does not have a fence for you to do your bands or a wall for you to throw weighted balls into? Are there certain exercises you prefer that are adaptable to varying conditions while others are not? How will these changing conditions impact your work? These are questions you are better off knowing the answers to *beforehand*, rather than finding them out when it matters most. Even within your preparation you must be *prepared* to make adaptations based on varying circumstances.

Twitter: @24Jono

Josh Zeid- Former MLB Pitcher, "All –World Team" World Baseball Classic 2017, MLB Rehab Pitching Coordinator

Pre-Game/Post Game Routines

If I were to tell you that Preparation and Routine are two of the most important concepts when it comes to having a long and prosperous career in baseball, would you believe me? Some would say "yes, absolutely" and some would say "maybe". I highly doubt if you are reading this book, you would say "no" to that question. Preparation and Routine begin in the offseason: at practice, in the weight room, and in the training room. This culminates in spring training and the season. If you skip steps along the way, you will tend to have more regrets on game day than you would had you stuck to your plan and managed your time wisely.

These steps consist of meeting throwing program benchmarks daily, completing mid-week bullpens, getting in your upper, lower, and total body lifts, conditioning, and getting a proper night's sleep. Making sure you take your non-game days as seriously as your game days will make your game days more normalized. Treating game days like they are of the utmost importance, the only day of the week that you train and work at 100% effort, then you put more pressure on yourself to succeed and be perfect on that day. Doing so makes life that much more challenging. Train and prepare for the outcome you expect, not the outcome you hope for.

A pitcher's pre-game warmup at the professional level is and should be multi-faceted. All of these pre-game activation techniques can be done by both starters and relievers. Relievers may have to work around the starting pitcher's time frame, as the starter has priority on his start day. However, your routine is also extremely important as a reliever.

The best pre-game routines start with proper nutrition and hydration the night before the outing through arriving at the ballpark. Once you arrive at the ballpark, eat a snack or small meal, let it settle, and then begin your routine. Efficiency is key here. For example:

5. Soak in the hot tub for 3-8 minutes. Any longer, and you risk becoming dehydrated. You can also choose to heat your lower half or throwing arm only.

6. Shower to rinse off the chemicals from the hot tub, and change into your uniform.

7. Go over the opposing team's lineup with the starting catcher and pitching coach.

   - Keep it simple. Try to pitch to your strengths, but it is just as important to know the offense's capabilities. Look for trends, but do not overcomplicate things.

8. 10-15-minute light bike ride to start activating your body. Get your heart rate going and break a sweat.

9. Get in a total body stretch with the Athletic Trainer. Some pitchers only get their upper body stretched out.

   - This step has multiple purposes. It loosens you up, allows the training staff to work out any hot spots, and also gives you 10-12 minutes of time to breathe, relax, and get in the zone before you go out to the field.

10. Jersey on and head outside.

   - Once you're outside, engage in a solid pre-game on-field warm up. These come from programs and techniques I used when I played, combined with methods and tricks I learned from other players that had success at the highest levels.

11. Engage in light callisthenic and static stretching. Check your surroundings. Get a feel for your cleats on the grass, and the feel of environment around you. The last thing you want to do is just walk outside and start throwing. Hear the sounds, feel the grass, walk to the bullpen mound and get comfortable toeing the rubber well before you even need to do it.

12. Perform a J-Band routine. These should be done with a purpose. I found that one time through the routine with 10-15 repetitions of each exercise listed below was enough to get my body going for that first plyocare throw.

    • Flies and reverse flies to overhead reach

    • Internal and external rotation

    • Elevated internal and external rotations

    • Split-stance overhead side bends

    • Reverse throws

- J-Band Pitch

- Elevated bicep curls

- Split stance overhead tricep extension

13. Plyocare warm up. I did not start using plyocare exercises until later in my career because they just were not available early on. However, I really loved what they did for me in terms of activation, arm path consistency, getting my lower half sequenced, and just overall fitness. One of my pre-start or pre-relief routines would look like the following

    - Reverse throws 1 x 10.

    - Constrained pivot pickoffs 1x10. This allows for timing and sequencing issues to be cleaned up early on.

    - Roll-ins 1 x 10. Focus on hip to shoulder separation.

    - Walk-in variations 2x 4 with blue, red, yellow, grey progression. Increase intensity here to create arm speed and begin to incorporate the delivery.

14. By now you have already made 38 plyocare throws, so your throwing program becomes all about feel, rhythm, and timing. You should not have to make as many throws early on, so getting into long toss should be fairly easy. "Listen to your arm" as Alan Jaeger always says. Get some air under the ball on your way out moving your feet. Make sure your arm is getting up and creating good extension out in front. On the way back in, increase the intensity, get into more of a leg lift in your crow hop and throw the ball on the line every 10-15 feet on your way in. Throw your changeups at 75-90' to help create arm speed on a pitch that requires it and spin your breaking ball at 60'.

15. Before your mound work, take a 3-5-minute break, towel off, and hydrate. Everyone's pre-game bullpen is going to look different and feel different. The idea behind your pre-game mound work is to get comfortable going down the slope, and work on timing and rhythm. Focus early on should be commanding the fastball low and away, then pitch to the quadrants: up and away, up and in, and low and in. Changeups and breaking balls should be thrown both in and out of the strike zone.

- I always threw 37 pitches. Out of the windup I threw 3 FB's middle, 3 FB's outside, 3 FBs inside, 3 CH's, and 6 alternating FB/CH. Out of the stretch I threw 3 FB's in, 3 FB's out, 3 SLs, and 5 FB/SL.

- I loved throwing my last 5 pitches of my pen out of my windup to the leadoff hitter. I'd **visualize** him standing in the batter's box, and I'd have my catcher call a sequence of pitches that I would have to complete.

16. My favorite part of a start day was the walk from the bullpen to the dugout. Take in the lights, chat with your catcher and pitching coach, and get in the zone. **Breathe. Believe in the work you did all week, and all that is left is to go out there and compete.**

So, you just went out and threw 6 innings of 0 run baseball. How do I cool down? **What is my post-game routine going to look like?**

I was told one time early in my playing days that when you come out of the game, you stay in the dugout and watch your team finish the inning you just exited. Then you watch the next half inning, at the very least. You are part of a team and you need to show the same amount of support to your teammates that they showed you.

Once you go into the clubhouse and you have access to your athletic trainer during the game, change out of your sweaty uniform and get into a clean and not-so sweaty shirt, and do your cool down exercises. This was my post-start routine:

1. Resisted manuals. 1-2 sets of 10/12 reps for the entire series.

2. D-cels. 2 sets of 12 with a 1 lb. ball.

3. Kettle bell holds and carry 2 x 20-yard holds

4. Forearm series: rice bucket, wrist curls, wrist rollers.

5. Cool down on the bike for about 15 minutes while hydrating.

Pre and Post game routines are extremely important. You do not have to be the best athlete in the room or the best pitcher on the field to always give 100% effort. If you prepare your mind and body every single day the right way, you can go into every contest with the utmost confidence knowing that you are ready no matter what the world throws at you.

Twitter: @Josh_Zeid14

Nick Sanzeri- MLB/MiLB/College Pitching Consultant- Pitching Coach- Mission College

#1 Most important thing for **Velocity Development**

FIND REPEATABLE MECHANICS- Consistent, healthy movement patterns

- Physical Screening (PT, Movement Specialists)

  o What are your deficiencies?

    ▪ **Develop a program to attack those weaknesses**

  o Re-screen every 2/3 weeks

Stable/Mobile Connections

  o All of our joints alternate between being *stable* and *mobile*

  o Examples:

STABLE	MOBILE
• Knee	• Hips
• Lumbar Spine	• T-Spine
• Scaps	• Shoulder
• Elbow	• Wrist

After you take care of ALL of your movement deficiencies… THEN you can do the fun stuff!

- Weighted baseballs

- Weightlifting

- Drill work

How to Improve Command

- **Focused** intent reps → CATCH PLAY

- Catch play: take pride in your catch play!

- Pitchers who have the best command throw with a purpose. From the first throw to the last throw—every throw is done with a purpose—whether that be throwing changeups in catch play or even focusing on a specific location during pulldowns… every throw must be done with a **PURPOSE.**

Twitter: @SanzeriBaseball Instagram: @sanzeribaseball

Rob Hill- MiLB Pitching Coordinator- Los Angeles Dodgers

Velocity Can Be Trained

For too long, the sports world hung their hat on the idea that talent was an untouchable and innate attribute only possessed by the genetically gifted. That idea has now since been refuted and there is nowhere it is more evident than in the rise of velocity development within the baseball training community. Technology has provided us with avenues to improve these long held "natural" attributes. Driveline baseball has long held the idea that velocity can be trained and that pitchers can improve beyond what they believed to be their genetic ceilings. Throwing hard, like anything, is a skill that can be learned with a combination of proper instruction, willingness to change, and often times sheer work ethic. Being someone who came into Driveline as a trainee in 2014 throwing around 83mph and then touching 90 less than a year later, I am a living example of how modern training can push people beyond where their "talent" would have gotten them. I foresee the baseball world continuing to move towards **data driven, objective** solutions to combat their problems. How well people can leverage research and technology and put that information into the hands of competent coaches is what will define successful baseball in the coming years. We have opened Pandora's box— there is no putting it all back together.

With gold standard motion capture data, we are now able to look at the totality of a pitcher's delivery, note any inefficiencies within it, and then build a custom-tailored program to help rectify that specific athlete's deficiencies. It is not a perfect science yet, and it is constantly iterated on, which is why Driveline baseball will continue to grow and succeed: the willingness to change. Too many people attach to one piece of the delivery, or one cue, or one mental model of proper mechanics, when in reality there are virtually infinite problems and solutions within a pitcher's delivery. **Driveline has no dogma.** We are constantly iterating and constantly evaluating and seeing how we can improve our methods. It is this openness to metamorphosis that will both continue to help in the success of Driveline and also improve the abilities of players to reason with their own preconceived notions in an effort to improve.

Twitter: @Berticushill Instagram: @Robapotamus

Dustin Pease- Former Professional Player-Founder - Lokation Nation- Author of "Lokation Nation's Guide to Commanding Locations"

Locate. Locate. Locate.

There are many questions surrounding what exactly high school baseball players should focus on in their own development process. The answer to that question I feel relies heavily on an individualized development program dependent on the goals and desires of said athlete. In regards to strength and mobility, I'll defer to the specialists in that regard. I will say, however, not every athlete should be lumped into the same bucket of workouts as another, especially pertaining to position-specific and goal-specific workouts. Each athlete has individual areas that need specific attention and the specificity to those certain areas requires further reflection by the designer.

High school pitchers are behind the eight ball when it comes to development. This means they will be forced into more intensity, effort, and raw output to produce high velocity in order to be recognized as an option to play at a higher level of the game. The same rules apply to collegiate level players hoping to play professionally. What does this mean you should do? Personally, I think there are a couple areas that require further thought on the process of the athlete. Being a fully functional pitcher in a baseball game requires an onslaught of skill coupled with raw intensity. A significant majority of amateur pitchers opt to sell out for higher velocity to appease the industry's admission factor— velocity. This leads to a bevy of unfortunate outcomes mainly leading to poor performance, less ability to learn new skills, and sadly, injury.

There is no harm in learning the importance, knowledge of pitching location, and its effect on hitters. There is no harm in learning that command is the single most important aspect in competing in a baseball game. Competing in a baseball game is different than advancing in baseball. The industry and culture do not do a quality job in valuing that aspect for aspiring pitchers. Make no mistake, however, Major League baseball pitchers possess equal and blended ability in terms of consistently executing pitches over others.

What should aspiring pitchers at the amateur level do?

1. Learn knowledge of location and that it's most important in strategizing. (EV - Effective Velocity)

2. Learn that the skill of command helps execute aforementioned knowledge.

3. Learn that velocity is merely an admission ticket to higher levels of play rather than a definition of success rate.

How do you train command?

1. Define it by your standard.

2. A guiding standard would be a 70% execution rate.

3. The standard is arbitrary to the user (you decide whether execution occurred)

4. Purposely do action always (first throw to final throw)

5. Test your ability under pressure.

What specifically should I do in my daily training to improve command?

DEFINE THE MECHANISM OF MOVEMENT.

1. LOCATE rather than throw. (mindset)

2. LOCATE daily.

3. LOCATE in high volume. (Lots of throws in block format - aka same location)

4. LOCATE at lesser intensity first.

5. LOCATE in intensity increments.

6. LOCATE under pressure in game like environments.

7. Prioritize the repetition of tasks over the repetition of movement.

8. Eliminate 'throwing' from your vocabulary. Throwing is a byproduct of locating.

Myelination is a term used to describe the insulation / ensheathment of an axon which reinforces the signal for certain procedures of the mind / body for specific tasks / movement. The less purpose / focus / analysis / adjustment we make rep to rep for a desired task, the less Myelin will be created around specific patterns to achieve explicit goals. The more the mind prioritizes and standardizes a task, the more myelin we will create en-route to reaching proficiency. The Myelin, or white matter in the brain, is what reinforces / supercharges our movements. This means that significant time spent LOCATING in high volumes (more throws) even at lesser intensity gives us the opportunity to move at higher rates of force due to Myelination. Myelination essentially fires signals faster (increased conduction velocity), and creates quicker movements through our schemes, even though we may feel like we are moving at same / similar effort levels. The more we allow our brain to navigate the same pattern, the faster it will fire signals through those patterns. Myelin is also built around purpose / task, the same way it won't exist without purpose. Neurons are built around our ability to not just throw a baseball, but to LOCATE the ball to where it needs to go. Every throw spent without purpose, is myelinating axons or brain signals that have no direction. Let's insulate tasked signals. Purpose your movement and optimize your movement fully to be functional in baseball games. TASK your movement. Command.

Twitter: @lokationnation Instagram: @lokationnation

arm pain

Arm soreness is a completely normal occurrence
for baseball players.
Throwing a baseball overhead is not a natural movement;
our body doesn't exactly love that we do it.
Throwing a baseball, especially at high velocities and at
high frequencies brings a ton of stress
on the major muscles involved— such as the rotator cuff,
the scapula, etc.

Too many young players undergo Tommy John surgery because of
their inability to properly prepare strengthen,
and recover their body and arm.

CONTENT CREATED BY PERRY QUARTUCCIO

169

ARM PAIN

We all know the typical "take an ibuprofen, rub some Icy Hot on it, and hold the elbow" routine to get rid of your arm soreness.

Pitchers: we've all done this and if you tell me you never have, you're lying.

We ALL know that there is a better to way to go about treating your arm and your body.
NSAIDS and topical pain relieving creams are not the answer!

First, you need to address the pain.
Is it soreness or sharp pain?

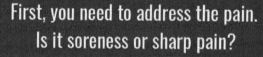

IF IT'S SORENESS, you can treat that accordingly and use many recovery modalities mentioned in this book.

IF IT'S A SHARP PAIN IN ANY AREA AROUND YOUR ARM, it's probably a good idea to see a specialized doctor.

CONTENT CREATED BY PERRY QUARTUCCIO

Lennon Richards- High Performance Trainer @ Baseball Development Group

PITCH DESIGN

The grip will always be the starting point of Pitch Design. Without the context of the grip, the data is pretty close to meaningless.

In terms of grips themselves, I find the fastball to be one of the most interesting. Since the fastball is the first pitch most learned, it can also be the one with the least time spent mastering or contextualizing. With a significant portion of our athletes, we'll find funky fastball grips that have stuck with them until the upper ranks of High School, College or even Pro. Simple things like their thumb positioning can be overlooked and end up hindering the shape and/or performance of their pitch.

An example of this is when an athlete presents with their thumb on the side of the ball instead of placing it at the bottom creating three even points of contact on the ball. By placing pressure on the side of the ball with the thumb, this can slightly shift the spin axis of the ball and result in a loss of spin efficiency. The loss of spin efficiency will result in less total movement of the pitch but can also present with a decrease in velocity on the pitch. So, grips, while very player specific, play a foundational role in the overall art of Pitch Design.

Twitter: @lennonrichards_

George Brown- Pitching Coach- St. John's University

INDIVIDUAL DEVELOPMENT AND FREEDOM

"We use a variety of developmental tools at St. John's. We have several players that use Driveline protocols (plyoballs, weighted balls), the Core Velocity Belt, Jaeger bands, and Crossover Symmetry Bands, in addition to Rapsodo, Motus, Blast Motion and Trackman. An important thing to note is that all of these products are just tools. We take pride here in the ability to provide a lot of freedom within your routine as a pitcher. Not all of our players use each of these tools, and that's the specific reason for having different options. I understand different training protocols will work for certain pitchers. Our players are expected to take their individual development seriously, and take accountability for their individual progression. There is a high level of importance put on the shoulders of each player to communicate with me if things are not working and when they need help. If a player comes in with no knowledge of what to do with tools or programming, I can give him things to do, no doubt. We do have a way of doing things here as a staff, but again, the freedom of finding what works for each individual is something that works very well."

"Line up! Give me 10 poles."

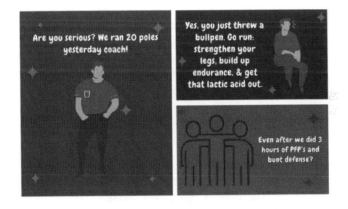

PITCHERS: STOP RUNNING POLES. NO MORE LONG-DISTANCE RUNNING!!!

This is a topic that seems to draw up a feud between baseball coaches. Baseball is a very "traditional" based sport, which is great, but sometimes these traditions are detrimental to a player's success. I know this debate is slowly reaching its end but it still pains me to hear or see that high school coaches are making their players run poles or run miles at a time on a daily practice basis. There seems to be this common belief that "flush runs" are beneficial for pitchers who have just thrown, and are used as a recovery modality. "Go run 10 poles, get rid of that lactic acid." We've all heard that before. Research and other experts have been debunking this common misbelief to do more harm than good.

David Aardsma- Former 9 Year MLB Veteran- Toronto Blue Jays Pitching Rehab Coordinator

How Should Our Pitchers Run?

There has been a debate going on for a long time now on the ideal running program in baseball. As long as I could remember, running in baseball was based around the concept of having your pitchers run as long and as far as possible. The idea behind this was very simple and, on the surface, it seemed to make sense. If our pitchers can run longer distances to condition their cardiovascular system and put themselves through the type of stresses it takes to run those long distances 'our pitchers will be able to pitch longer into games'. That was the traditional mindset. At Rice University when our coach thought the pitchers were getting too soft (or honestly, he just wanted to get rid of us for a while), we would have to run the 3-mile loop around the campus. In pro ball, I still remember the standard 18 pole running program after practice in spring training. At the beginning of every spring training the pitchers would dread the standard timed mile run. It was a normal part of being a pitcher to run long distance and it was a part of who we were.

One of the biggest advantages of the long endurance running was the mental component. If the pitcher can mentally will themselves to push through the barriers of these long distances, then when they get tired and they face a tough situation late in the ball game, they will be prepared and ready to fight through it just like they do in training. Without a doubt, there is a huge mental component to running long distances and forcing yourself into a tougher mindset but this question comes into play: are we breaking down our pitchers physically in the process?

Before we dive into the process of pitching, we need to talk about Aerobic vs Anerobic training. The Aerobic energy system basically means "With Oxygen". The type of exercises that fall into this category are slow-twitch movements like jogging, jump roping, and using a rowing machine. Anerobic on the other hand means "Without Oxygen". Exercises in this category generally involve fast-twitch, short bursts of energy like sprints, plyometrics, and weightlifting. Now to understand how our pitchers should train, we need to dive into the pitcher's main task: pitching.

In its simplest form, pitching is a set of quick movements spaced apart by 12-20 seconds breaks. Our goal as Major League pitchers and coaches is to have our pitchers throw 14 or fewer pitches per inning and for that pitcher to last as long into the game as possible. For relievers, we apply the same rule but we typically have them throw 1-3 innings. Our goal for our starters is to have them throw 100+ pitches a game. While on the surface it may appear that we want our pitchers to train aerobically because the Starter may throw 100 pitches over a three-hour time span, however, in reality, it is the same as 100 quick, short, powerful sprints which activates the anaerobic system. So now, we need to ask the question, should we be training the classic old school way or train how our pitchers actually perform?

This is where old school baseball has finally caught up with new school concepts. While there is a mental benefit to long distance aerobic training, that doesn't mean we cannot gain the same benefits in shorter anerobic sprints. Overtime, the more you train your slow-twitch aerobic system, the slower your anerobic fast-twitch system becomes. **We need to be training our pitchers in the same way that they perform in games, with quick burst movements that challenge their bodies and prepare them for the rigors of the game atmosphere.**

Twitter: @TheDA53

176

Fielding

Sophomore Year- High-School

HERE'S A PIC OF ME PLAYING SHORT. WHY ARE
MY PANTS SO TIGHT?

*In this chapter, you'll read about some of the intricacies of
defense with information ranging from two infield coaches, one
outfield coach, and two catching coaches. Please keep in mind that
I have never played outfield or caught in my entire life...*

Sean Travers- Founder of 64 Club

"Middle Infielders Must Be Able to Play Both Sides of
The Bag"

When I was 14-years-old, I hadn't played many
positions other than **SHORTSTOP.** My favorite
players were Alfredo Griffin and Tony Fernandez
because they were the Blue Jays SS when I was growing
up. The place I wanted to visit most in the world was
San Pedro de Macoris, Dominican Republic because
that's where they were from.

Sure, I liked Damaso Garcia, the Blue Jays' **SECOND
BASEMAN,** but he didn't play the position I played. I
was a shortstop. That is, until I met Denny Doyle at a
Doyle Baseball School.

When the coaches broke the campers into specific
defensive groups, the 2B and SS were grouped together.

I didn't think much of it at first. In his introduction, Denny asked the group what position we played. There were about 10 kids in the group and 6 said shortstop and 4 said second base. Denny had a weird smile on his face and he responded, "From now on you are all **MIDDLE INFIELDERS. YOU HAVE TO BE ABLE TO PLAY BOTH SIDES OF THE BAG.**"

If you think about most youth teams, the SS is usually the best athlete (or the coach's son) and the 2B is a smaller gritty-type player (a gamer). The SS spends the next 3 or 4 years playing on natural ability not really working on their skills and the 2B works at a position where they are throwing the ball less than 60 feet most of the time. Both scenarios are terrible for a player's development. It is easy to say all SS can play 2B, but not all 2B can play SS. The reason for this is SS is viewed as a much more physically demanding position. I agree that usually the SS has a better arm but that is no excuse for the 2B not to be able to play on the left side. How many times do you think guys like David Eckstein were told they could only play 2B?

Second Base, on the other hand, is a much more skill-oriented (learned movements) position. Everything at 2B is backwards and fights against what your body wants to naturally do. Sure, if you put a SS at 2B he will make the routine play but remember, turning the double play is ultimately a middle infielder's job and if the SS has not worked on their turns and feeds from second, they will not be very good at it.

So, what I learned from Denny that day was even if I wasn't spending much time at second base in the games,

I needed to learn and work on all aspects of that position as well. In college and professional baseball, I played 80% of the time at 2B and 20% of the time at SS.

<u>Second Baseman</u>

Like I said before, youth coaches put the small gritty players at second base. A lot of times, these players are just happy to be in the lineup and are happy to be at 2B because they are intimidated by the longer throw at SS. The first thing they need to work on is their **arm strength**.

How do you work on arm strength? (not in any particular order of importance)

1. Overall strength will help (get in the gym or body weight exercises if your younger).

2. J-Bands-Learn the program and do it religiously.

3. Weighted Balls Find a good weighted ball program.

4. Long Toss- Throw as far as you can then finish with as hard as you can.

5. MOST IMPORTANTLY-Take at least 80% of your ground balls at SS and throw across the diamond. Even if you have to one-hop the ball to first base, make sure there is no arc in your throw.

Arm strength can be improved! That being said, all you can do is maximize your potential. Some of the best MLB SS of all time Ozzie Smith, Omar Vizquel, and Tony Fernandez had below average arms. How did they play SS in the big leagues? They worked on a style that suited them. They attacked every ball, had incredibly quick hands and feet, threw from various angles, and were extremely creative.

<u>Shortstops</u>

Being gifted athletically can be a curse (so can being the coach's son). I have encountered many gifted SS that are not fundamentally sound and they survived high school baseball on these gifts alone. They sit back on ground balls and their footwork and hands-on double play turns are very pedestrian. They rely on great arm strength to throw out less athletically gifted high school runners.

The lack of work on the fundamentals and skill is multiplied when they move to second base because now momentum is working against them.

When a 2B feeds the SS on a double play, the natural footwork (what feels comfortable) is right foot in front of left foot. The problem with this is when you go to feed, your hips are in the way. The correct way to field this ball is attack with your left foot so your hips are already pointing at 2B. If you have not worked hard on this, I guarantee it won't happen, especially in a game-time scenario.

Momentum is the key to turning the double play and at SS, that is very easy. At 2B, if you come across the bag to turn it, your momentum will take you towards the pitcher's mound. After catching the ball on your right foot, you must get your left foot moving toward first base. If you step back to turn it, natural momentum will take you toward right field. Once again, it will take **countless** practice reps to train your body to move toward first base.

The power feed from 2B is a powerful tool to get the ball to the SS quickly on a double play. Once again, if the player has not practiced this many times it is not something that they can naturally go to in a game. If they do, it will probably result in a poor feed.

The point of this is: **YOU ARE NO LONGER A SHORTSTOP OR A SECOND BASEMAN YOU ARE NOW A MIDDLE INFIELDER**. That being said, coaches and players, please make sure you work equal amounts from SS and 2B on double play turns and feeds. I also recommend that you take the majority of your ground balls from the left side when you are throwing to first base. Not much is accomplished from taking ground balls at 2B and flipping it 45 feet to the first baseman.

Twitter: @sixfourclub

Tim DeJohn- MiLB Infield Coach- Baltimore Orioles

Food for Thought

- My opinion: No right or wrong answers

- There are NO absolutes

- What's the most efficient way to get the job done with least margin of error?

- Things to consider:

  o What works?

  o What can the player physically perform?

  o Make fundamentals/drills "your own" for what fits into your system

- Be yourself!

Fielding Position

WIDE BASE

- 3 ways to lower body

- Will vary depending on the player

- Feet are roughly 1 foot wider than shoulder width

- Allows for "playing low" which sets up for success

Photo Adopted from Pixabay

- Eliminates blind spots
- Better glove positioning

GLOVE DISTANCE

- ➤ NOT "out in front"
- ➤ Like to use the cue "handshake distance"
- ➤ Allows player to see their glove and the ball
- ➤ Wide base assists in glove positioning

BUTT HIGH

- ➤ Weight into ball of feet, sets up for post-catch footwork
- ➤ Help keep a flat back and chest down
- ➤ Allows for waist hinge that sets up glove positioning
- ➤ Creates good vision
- ➤ Low butt:
  - Weight goes into heels
  - Field ball deeper, can't adjust
  - Chest comes up, affects vision

FIELD BALL ON LEFT SIDE

- ➤ Where your glove is
- ➤ Allows you to see ball with both eyes. "See it in."
- ➤ Creates opportunity for adjustability
- ➤ Sets up for good transfer
- ➤ Once ball gets to middle/right side, turn it over into a backhand

GLOVE POSITION

- ➤ Essentially field with one hand
- ➤ Palm to 2 o'clock
- ➤ Allows for the ball to stick in the pocket
- ➤ Natural hand position: loose
- ➤ Palm to 12 o'clock
    - o Ball can roll up glove
    - o Creates stiffness

Twitter: @DeJohn_5

OF
Darren Fenster- Minor League Outfield and Baserunning Coordinator- Boston Red Sox. Founder/CEO of Coaching Your Kids, LLC. Sport Development Team- USA Baseball

THE LAST LINE OF DEFENSE

Over the last few years, no skill in our game has transformed more than hitting. With new ways to evaluate swings, combined with more aggressive approaches to hitting the ball over the shift instead of around it, hitters are doing more damage than ever. For all that has changed in the batter's box, there is a very important corresponding fact that we need to acknowledge: outfield play has never been more important than it is today.

Every year as a manager, usually on the day when we are teaching our players the pop-fly priority team fundamental, I would gather everyone together and explain to them that when the ball went in the air, they needed to become Dennis Rodman. A confused look usually overcame the entire group, not knowing for sure who exactly Rodman was.

Before he became "that guy with all the tattoos" and before he was "that guy who became friends with North Korea's dictator" (as our young players vaguely recognized him), Dennis Rodman was arguably the best rebounder in NBA history, carving out a Hall-of-Fame career by doing the dirty work on the court that few would ever embrace. When the basketball was shot in the air, Rodman expected to get the rebound. Every single time. And THAT'S the approach all great outfielders have; when the ball goes in the air, they expect to catch it.

There are three main priorities when it comes to outfield play, and the first is a simple one: EFFORT. Go. Get. The. Ball. Without effort, an outfielder can't even be average. With effort, an outfielder will always give himself a chance to make a play. All of the extra bases are in the outfield, and nothing shuts down the extra base easier or better than simply effort to get on the baseball. The harder an outfielder goes after a ball, the sooner a baserunner or third-base coach has to make the decision on whether or not to stretch an extra 90 feet or send the runner around.

The second priority of outfield play is a mental one: ENGAGEMENT. We want all of our players, no matter the position but especially our outfielders, to engage to the pitch, the play, and the game. In the Major Leagues, on average, roughly 300 pitches are thrown per game. That means for 150 of them, our players are out in the field playing defense and are expected to lock in mentally on every single one. That means they are timing out their pre-pitch to be ready to move to the best of their ability if the ball is hit their way.

We expect our outfielders to be engaged to the play. Whenever the ball is put in play, and many times when it's not, there is always somewhere for everyone on the field to be. When players are focused on their specific job at hand, they are in the correct position, doing the right thing. The final piece of engagement is with the game. Depending on the score, the situation, or the inning, the variables of the game will dictate our players' decisions offensively and, in this case, defensively. When our outfielders are engaged to the game, they know where to throw the ball, when to dive for a ball, or when to play it safe.

And lastly, the final priority of outfield play is OWNERSHIP, where we want our players to take pride in perfecting their craft in becoming the best defenders they can be. This is a two-pronged focal point, the first of which takes place during drill work. Our practice routines are designed in a way to only have one or two specific things to work on as we progress through our drill packages. When players truly take ownership, their drill work is laser-focused on the things they are working on and they can't help but get better.

The second part of ownership is found during batting practice... on the outfield grass. Without question, the most important part of an outfielder's day is when they work live during BP. There is no drill that offers a better rep than what an outfielder can get during batting practice. It's as close to a game rep as there is, allowing for outfielders to get consistent with their pre-pitch timing, clean up their reads and breaks, and perfecting their routes to the ball. How an outfielder approaches batting practice will determine whatever they will become.

Many coaches have long tried to "hide" a productive bat in the outfield, thinking that they could sacrifice defense in favor of offense. Well with the direction the game is going, that strategy probably isn't the smartest one in this day and age. For outfield is truly the last line of defense.

Twitter: @CoachYourKids

C

Todd Coburn-

THE "BIG 3" OF RECEIVING:

There are several components to being a good receiving catcher but, in my opinion, there are three main aspects of the skill that can make the biggest difference in performance. I call them the "Big 3," meaning the three most important things you or your catchers should be doing to be successful at receiving.

They are:

1. Be on time (the key is being relaxed and utilizing a pre-pitch mitt move in the direction or area of the anticipated pitch location).

2. Manipulate the mitt. Moving the mitt toward the strike zone whenever possible. You will move it sometimes more than others depending on pitch location.

3. Give the umpire a consistent look both with the movements you or your catchers make and the mitt position (horizontal or flat mitt position is ideal).

THE "BIG 3" OF BLOCKING:

There are several things a catcher must do to be a consistently successful blocking catcher but the most important or what I call the "Big 3" of blocking are:

1. Mindset. The catcher needs to always expect the ball to be in the dirt and have a no-fear attitude.

2. Proper Transition into Blocking Position. The catcher must utilize the correct transition technique depending on the depth of the pitch – Drop/Replace OR Fold/Attack. If the pitch is almost catchable, the catcher will typically drop or replace. If the pitch is short, the catcher will typically cut down the distance where they drop and where the ball is hitting the ground by folding or "attacking" the ball.

3. Proper Blocking Position. Sometimes you or your catcher will be on one knee, sometimes on two knees. The bottom line is do what you've got to do to "catch it" with your belly button. Hips are down, chest over the top (changes on depth of pitch meaning if it is short, you're more upright, if it's deep, you're more over the top), mitt deep blocking the "five hole" and chin tucked.

THE "BIG 4" OF THROWING:

There are four main components to being a good throwing catcher. I call them the "Big 4" of Throwing (as opposed to the "Big 3" of almost every other skill) and they include:

1. Mindset (Be confident and anticipate)

2. Quick Hands (Let the ball come to you, move both arms in straight line)

3. Quick Feet (utilize the correct method and keep the step short)

4. Arm Strength (higher velocity for shorter flight time) / Throwing Mechanics (consistency and injury prevention).

CHARACTERISTICS OF A SUCCESSFUL CATCHER:

The list of required characteristics or qualities needed to be a successful catcher is long. If a coach has a group of catchers in front of them and they are trying to decide who their starter is going to be, here are what I feel are the top four qualities, in order of importance:

1. Leadership qualities

2. Mental toughness

3. Physical toughness & tools

4. Skills & Responsibilities

To clarify, yes, you need to be able to receive pitches consistently, yes, you need to be able to block with no fear and yes, you need to be able to make the throw to second base. You need to be able to handle your responsibilities, but if a coach has a group of catchers in front of them that have similar skill sets, the above list of qualities is typically what most coaches will go by to determine who will be their catcher.

Twitter: @TheCatchingGuy Instagram: @the_catching_guy

Micheal Thomas- MiLB Catching Coordinator-
Minnesota Twins

1. How do professional catchers warm-up pre-game?

With how the game is going, everyone has come to the realization that we should approach most aspects with individuality. When you look across the board at professional baseball players, they all have some form of warmup preparation that they partake in to get them ready to go for the game. For catchers specifically, we try to approach this space with the same intent of individuality with a touch of specificity to who (pitcher) they are going to be catching. I think most catchers go through their warmup for that exact purpose: to "warmup". If we allow our warmup to be tailored to the starting pitcher, you can better prepare yourself to be successful in the game.

Think of it this way: for hitters, we understand that if they are going to see 95 mph with some carry, it would be beneficial for us as hitters to see that prior to the game to be best prepared. This goes the same for catchers. If we are going to catcher 95 mph with carry, we should see that prior to going to catch with that pitcher.

Every pre-game routine should consist of receiving, blocking and throwing (no particular order). Start by replicating the pitch with the resources you have available to receive. Work multiple locations to cover all areas of the zone. From there, work on blocking the primary breaking ball to allow the body to react to centering up the shape of the pitch. Lastly, make sure to work footwork into the equation as well to multiple bases.

2. What advice do you give to the guys you work with who are ultimately trying to make it to the next level?

"You need to have a desire to succeed at a level that will motivate you to work diligently with a purpose."

Everyone is trying to make it to the next level, and as a player, you need to be aware of that. At the end of the day, skills and success pays dividends, but how we are getting there is also important. You need to have a desire to succeed at a level that will motivate you to work diligently with a purpose. Anyone can "try" or "practice", but, having a purpose and desire about what you are doing is imperative. That's where real development and growth comes from and can ultimately push you further and further in your career.

Another thing I tell guys is they need to be really good at what they are supposed to be really good at on and off the field. Being "flashy" only comes so often, but being able to master the things they need to do consistently is key.

3. What can you say to HS/college catchers who want to play professionally?

It's important to **understand what makes you good**. If you have the chance to potentially get to that level, it's going to take a lot of discipline within yourself to understand what makes you good. With social media in today's world, we can get lost in trying to accomplish everything or be like someone else. Be who you are and allow yourself to do what makes you good as a player. A phrase I say often is: "Have the ability to master simplicity." I think that, as players, we get lost in what it truly is that we are trying to accomplish. By keeping it simple and having the ability to master this, we will layer on and grow to our foundation.

4. What does the life of a professional catcher entail?

At all levels, being a catcher is not easy. We usually are the first ones to the park and last ones to leave. That doesn't change in professional baseball. You get to the field early to start preparing for the day. Whether that's physically to catch that evening or game-planning to face the opposing team. Over the course of 140-162 games, it can get monotonous, but having **the ability to be rooted and disciplined in your routine** will make the process fun.

Having this ability to know when to dial in and when to "unload" is key. The guys who never take time for themselves or families are the ones that burn out mentally and physically. While the ultimate goal is to make it to the Big Leagues, having the ability to enjoy your ride there is the difference between the guys who make it and who don't—the ones who stick and who don't. At the end of the day, we play a game and we have to remember that it's supposed to be fun.

Twitter: @Micheal_T42

Recovery

RECOVERY

Recovery is paramount to a player's success.
Work hard, recover harder.

Two most important aspects of recovery:
nutrition and sleep.
Be sure to read up on what the experts have to
say about that in this chapter.

Some other recovery modalities:

- "Spot" Icing
- Cold water immersion/ Cryotherapy
- Electronic Stimulation (E-Stim)
- Deep Tissue Massage/ Foam Rolling
- Dry Needling/ Cupping Therapy
- Stretching/ Mobility

Unpopular opinion: Icing doesn't help arm soreness.
Why are you icing after you throw?
Icing is beneficial to reducing inflammation.
Usually good for post-injury

CONTENT CREATED BY PERRY QUARTUCCIO

My Take

My take on recovery is this: find what works best for
you and run with it. Establish a solid recovery routine
that allows your body to **feel good** and **perform** at
your highest level.

Personally, I enjoyed **deep tissue massages** and **foam rolling**. I also loved when athletic trainers performed active muscle release techniques on me (**AMR**). Another thing I enjoyed doing: **yoga**. Yoga would make me feel rejuvenated, more mobile, and more relaxed. To this day, I implement a yoga routine whenever I start to feel stressed.

Recovery routines should be applied on a day-to-day basis, especially if you're playing at a high level. If your body doesn't recover, you have a higher risk of injury, you will most likely not perform at your best, and your body will break down quicker. Reiterated again, PRIORTIZE YOUR SLEEP AND NUTRITION.

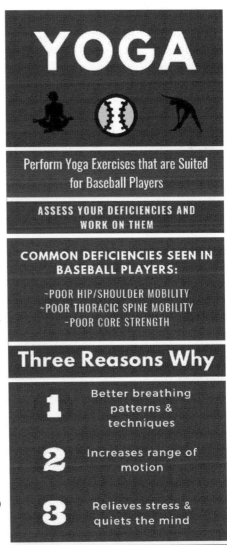

YOGA

Perform Yoga Exercises that are Suited for Baseball Players

ASSESS YOUR DEFICIENCIES AND WORK ON THEM

COMMON DEFICIENCIES SEEN IN BASEBALL PLAYERS:

~POOR HIP/SHOULDER MOBILITY
~POOR THORACIC SPINE MOBILITY
~POOR CORE STRENGTH

Three Reasons Why

1 Better breathing patterns & techniques

2 Increases range of motion

3 Relieves stress & quiets the mind

CONTENT CREATED BY PERRY QUARTUCCIO

Mike Duffy and Carolann Duffy, two experts in their field, talk about the importance of sleep and nutrition and how to improve those aspects.

Thrive Spine and Sports discusses the idea of Cryotherapy and its proposed benefits in this section, too.

Tommy Eveld talks about his experiences with recovery and why it is crucial in professional baseball.

Again, find out what works for you and run with it!

Background Information

At Thrive Spine and Sports Rehab, we utilize modern techniques and equipment to maximize our effectiveness treating the active population and athletes. We offer acupuncture, chiropractic, physical therapy, and whole-body cryotherapy. Over time, we have been able to develop and improve treatment plans geared towards people that are very active and athletes through the combination of all of our modalities. These treatment plans are then broken down by the athlete population we are working on, the specific injury, or to speed up recovery and prevent injury. Baseball players are a group we often work on with elbow or shoulder problems due to the nature of overhead throwing. We will combine physical therapy and acupuncture for the acute patient that needs help with recruiting certain muscles to prevent an injury from occurring again. Chiropractic care is often added into the plan, seeing as the neck can often take a lot of wear and tear during the throwing motion as well. Some patients utilize all of the treatments we have available to help them recover from training faster and more efficiently, and to reduce pain and chance of injury while they continue to train and play.

Cryotherapy

Whole-Body Cryotherapy is a phenomenal tool when it comes to treating patients! It has applications to help with physical recovery after a hard training session to treat acute and chronic injuries and even some diseases. At Thrive, we believe in providing the BEST when it comes to all of our treatments. We have done countless hours of research on the topic and looked into the differences between the systems. There are two main systems, one that is nitrogen based, (Cryo-Sauna), and one that is electric based, (Cryo-Chamber AKA Cryotherapy). At Thrive, we have an electric machine that has benefits that go above and beyond the nitrogen-based systems.

With the nitrogen-based system, or Cryo-Sauna, the patient walks into a cylinder that typically covers from the shoulders down to the feet. The patient's head and neck are outside of the sauna because nitrogen obviously cannot be inhaled. Also, the patient has to rotate every 30 seconds or so for the 3-minute session to prevent burns, which is very common with nitrogen systems.

Electric cryotherapy is a very different experience. The chamber sits at -170 to -190 Degrees Fahrenheit ALL DAY! Patients put on gloves, face masks, slippers, and ear muffs; then they step into the machine for roughly 3 minutes. This machine is fully enclosed, much like a giant walk in freezer-- just much colder. With a full glass front, patients can look through to keep an eye on the timer or watch something on TV. So, with this system the entire head and neck is exposed to the subzero temperatures without the need to move or rotate. Just stand still and get cold. When it comes to the research, electric cryotherapy is often called cryostimulation because of the improved effects it has on metabolic and inflammatory responses within the body due to the ability to get the head and brain cold. It also produces the same enhanced recovery effects of the Cryo-Sauna (nitrogen-based system) from exercise and injuries.

Baseball players undergo a lot of trauma and inflammation in their throwing arm every time they play, and pitchers induce even more. With our Cryo-Chamber, we can help to quickly reduce the body's inflammatory response, especially in the neck and shoulders, which can reduce pain and speed up the recovery of the athlete. Speeding up the recovery allows the athlete back on the field at 100%, preparing them for the next day for practice/ game. So, at Thrive, we recommend this to all of our baseball players to assist them to always be at their best!

Instagram:
@thrivespineandsportsrehab

Tommy Eveld- Miami Marlins Organization RHP

"In my opinion, this could be the most important topic in the book. Every single topic being covered is based around recovery. If you are not capable of pitching or playing on a day to day basis, teams will not want you. As a relief pitcher, I get to the field every day and I ask myself "What do I need to do to be able to pitch tonight?" The only thing that matters is availability. If you are hurt, or so sore you cannot perform on a regular basis, you simply will not have a job. There are so many different tools, machines, and activities you can do for recovery. It is up to the player to talk with the trainer and identify how you are feeling, what the trainer recommends, and how your body reacts to what you do.

An in-season routine, for a reliever at least, has to be built around being ready to pitch every night. This also comes down to knowing your body and the best way to know your body is to experiment and take notes. Your notes should include what you did to get sore (pitching, workout, running, or even hiking/something off the field), what you are doing to try and relieve soreness, and the timing of it. Did you lift weights before the game or after? Did you run extra before the game or after? Did you get fascial scraping or cupping therapy before the game or after?

Once you make a note of what and when you did something, make a note of how you feel after, and how you feel the next day before you start doing anything. Again, I cannot stress enough to learn your own body through trial and error. At the lower levels in the minor leagues, they have strict rules on not throwing back to back days, not throwing back to back after a certain number of pitches, and how many times you are allowed to throw off the mound in a week. This is the perfect time to try and develop a routine. If you know for a fact that you are not pitching the next day and your arm is usually sore the day after you pitch, implement a change in your regimen to try to get your arm feeling ready to go. Another thing to be careful of is to not do too much. Sometimes, doing nothing is better than doing too much and fatiguing your muscles more."

Sleep

Carolann Duffy- BBA, AFAA, HLC, IIN Certified -

Owner Mike Duffy's Personal Training

'Those in the game of baseball have broken down almost everything in the quest for high level athletic achievement. And that can take the form of better nutrition, weight training, mental training, video technology, and progressive teaching concepts specific to the different skill sets required. But rarely do coaches talk about proper sleeping habits, which may be among the most important aspects of athletic performance" **LOU PAVLOVICH, JR.** Editor/Collegiate Baseball

Benefits of good quality sleep:

*Allows the body to recover from physical stress

*Makes athletes less prone to injuries

*Athletic performance improves

*Accelerates the building of muscle, strength, and endurance

*Rested athletes are faster and more accurate

*Growth hormones are reduced during sleep

Adverse effects from lack of sleep:

*Studies show that mild sleep deprivation reduces reaction time

*Fatigue may impair strike-zone judgment (Kutscher, Song, Wang, Upender, & Malow, 2013).

*MLB player's sleepiness can predict his longevity in the league (Kutscher et al., 2013).

How many hours should an athlete sleep?

Based on circadian rhythm, during the hours of 10pm to 2am the body experiences physical repair and during 2am to 6am the body experiences mental repair (but you must be sleeping). This is why it is critical to sleep from at least 10pm to 6am every night as often as possible. However, athletes need more than 8 hours of sleep. Many elite athletes including Venus Williams, Roger Federer, and LeBron James have stated that they sleep 10 hours per night.

Justin Verlander is considered to be the Astros' Sleep Guru:

> "It was early May 2018 and Alex Bregman, the Houston Astros' star third baseman, had only one home run on the season. His teammate Justin Verlander, one of the best pitchers of this generation, noticed Bregman's low power and hints of fatigue, and asked
>
> how many hours Bregman had slept the night before. 'Six,' Bregman answered. And his normal amount? 'Six', as well. The responses bewildered Verlander. He promptly told Bregman, 25, that he slept at least 10 hours a night and said Bregman should start getting more hours himself. "I felt like that's overdoing it," Bregman said. "You shouldn't sleep that much. "Then I started sleeping that much and, next thing you know, I hit 30 homers after that." (Wagner, NY Times, 2019)."

How to improve quality sleep:

*Sleep in total darkness (turn off all lights and use black out shades)

*Unplug all electronics

*Put cell phone on airplane mode

*No TV/computer 2 hours prior to bed

*Write down worries/to do list

*Eat right for your blood type to avoid blood sugar crashes during the night

*Avoid caffeine/sugar (especially after 12pm)

*Avoid alcohol (especially around bedtime)

*Avoid food additives and chemicals

"My family has called me the "sleep nazi" for over 20 years because I learned early on that sleep has a direct impact on daily performance. As the research indicates, sleep is so important for all of us, but even more so for athletes. Good luck to you in your baseball career."

Instagram: @carolannduffy

MY HACK

Although Carolann Duffy stated above that it's **ideal** to unplug from all electronics before going to bed. One can completely understand why this is beneficial, but, one thing I found that helps me sleep better is when I wear Blue Light Blocking Glasses. Our computer screens and our phone screens emit blue light. Supposedly, a lot of exposure to blue light may cause irritated eyes and hinders your ability to release melatonin, which proceeds to disrupt your sleep. While there is not a ton of empirical research done on this, this is something that I have found works for me. Perhaps it's all in my head or it's just a hoax, I don't know. Regardless, I feel as if I have an easier time falling asleep when I do wear the glasses before bed, opposed to when I don't wear them. For OPTIMAL sleep, it is certainly better to unplug electronics completely and it's something I definitely want to work on. Being a college student and living in a technology-demanding generation makes this adjustment difficult.

Something I found that works for me too—breathing. With my new discovery of meditative breathing, I realized I can nap at any time in the day with absolutely no problem, as well as shut down all of my thoughts that sometimes creep into my head late at night. There are so many different breathing techniques out there that you can use. Again, this entire book revolves around finding what works best for you or your children. The breathing technique I use to fall asleep easier is called the '4-7-8' (See "Mental Performance"). Inhale for 4 seconds, hold the breath in your lungs for 7 seconds, and then comes a long, deep exhale for 8 seconds. I put emphasis on the exhale only because I enjoy feeling the stress, the thoughts, and all of that negative energy leave my body. Cliché to say, sure, however, this helps me shut down when I need to. I encourage you to try this when you need help catching those Z's or even when you can't seem to quiet all of the thoughts that may enter your mind.

Nutrition

From the start of high school, I was this nutrition freak. At 14 years old, I used to follow this trainer and nutritionist I found on YouTube. His name was Brad Gouthro. He's an entrepreneur and the owner of Live Lean Fitness. I was eating omelets in the morning, meal prepping salads for lunch, and having chicken, rice, and broccoli dinners. I would go grocery shopping by myself and get all of the necessary whole foods and healthy snacks I could get (with Mom's debit card, of course). Everyone thought I was a weirdo. My friends used to make fun of me because I was the only kid at the table eating a salad. I used to crave sweets a lot, so I would make one of Brad's nutritious recipes: sweet potato cookies. These cookies may not look so appetizing, but they were phenomenal. Looking back, I admire my willpower to not eat unhealthy, processed foods at such a young age and in my high school environment. To get to the point, when you get to high school and you actually start to care about your baseball performance, you come to realize that proper nutrition is important. My question is: do you really? Are you really eating healthy and being cautious of what you put into your body? It may be time to self-reflect and ask yourself if you are truly making sure your nutrition is on point.

Summer Salad

- Greens Blend

- Strawberries, Grapes, Oranges

- Grilled Chicken

- Almonds, Pecans, Cashews

- Sugar-free Raspberry Vinaigrette

Sweet Potato Cookies

Here's a sample grocery list I use:

THINGS TO BUY AT THE GROCERY STORE

FRUITS

BLUEBERRIES
RASPBERRIES
BANANAS
PINEAPPLE
AVOCADOS

VEGETABLES

PEPPERS
BROCCOLI
CAULIFLOWER
SPINACH
KALE
MUSHROOMS
ZUCCHINI

FISH & MEAT

CHICKEN BREAST
GROUND TURKEY
GROUND BEEF- GRASS FED
STEAK
SALMON

SNACKS

WHEY PROTEIN
PEANUT BUTTER
KIND BARS
CHIA SEEDS

DAIRY

EGGS
ALMOND MILK
GREEK YOGURT

DRINKS

Mike Duffy- Certified Personal Trainer- Holistic Lifestyle Coach- AAHFRP Post Rehab Certified- WNPF National Powerlifting Champion- Former Natural Mr. America

Nutrition for Baseball

When it comes to eating for performance, you have to make sure that you are only consuming foods that will improve performance, not impede it. High level ballplayers need high octane foods. You wouldn't put cheap gas in an Indy 500 car on race day, would you?

The absolute best foods to consume are whole foods. Whole foods are best defined as foods that contain only one ingredient; they do not need nutrition labels. Some examples would be an apple, broccoli, steak, avocado, spinach, fish, etc. The more ingredients on a food label, the worse it is for you. Also, if you can eat organic versions of these foods, that would be even better.

Whole foods are not processed or minimally processed meaning they will contain a high nutrition content. The less processed a food is, the higher the nutritional value it will have (high octane gas). Organic whole foods are even higher in nutritional value because they do not contain any added herbicides, pesticides, hormones, or antibiotics. These are added to some whole foods especially if they are not labeled organic. Chemicals in your foods will inhibit your health and performance.

Once you make a commitment to eating for improved performance by following a whole food nutrition plan or an organic whole food nutrition plan you have to know what foods to eat. How much protein, carbohydrates and fats do you need? These are called macro nutrients.

Macros

Finding your perfect macronutrient profile is not easy. Some people do great on a high protein diet, some do great on a high fat diet, and some do great on a high carbohydrate diet. The key is to discover which one is best for you.

The easiest way to find your perfect macronutrient profile is to start with a balanced diet. It is best to start with a 50% carbohydrate, 30% protein, and 20% fat profile. If you follow this and you feel great, then this is what is working best for you. However, if you follow this profile and you are not feeling your best, you will need to adjust your foods. You might need more protein and fat and less carbs or vice versa. Try both ways and see which one makes you feel the best. You have to listen to your body. It does not matter what your doctor, nutrition guru, or expert says: if you are following their advice and your body doesn't feel optimal, their advice is wrong for you. Listen to **your** body!

Pre and Post Game Meals

Let's get one thing straight: if you are not eating correctly year-round it does not matter what you put into your body before a game—it will not help. You need to be eating for peak performance every day, every meal, building your body's strength, health, and level of performance all of the time. If you have two athletes who have the same athletic level, the one who eats correctly year-round will have a likelier chance of outperforming the one who *only* eats correctly pre-game.

Pre-game meals

It takes 2-4 hours to digest carbohydrates and 4-6 hours to digest proteins and fats so an effective pre-game meal should take place about 4 hours prior to game time so that all your macro nutrients are there ready for peak performance. If you eat too much too close to game time, your digestive system and muscular system will be competing for blood supply and you will have incomplete digestion and a lower blood supply to your brain and muscles at game time. Here is an example of a whole food pre-game meal:

- Grilled chicken 6-8 ounces (add herbs and spices for taste)

- Rice- about 1-1 ½ cup

- Mixed vegetables 1-2 cups sautéed in olive oil

- 1 cup chopped pineapple

This is a great meal to have about 4 hours pre-game. Once you eat this and play, you will want to take notice of your energy levels and how you felt while playing. If you felt great, then you hit it spot on. If you were dragging or not able to focus, you will have to make adjustments to your pre game meal. Maybe you need a little more carbs and fats and less protein. This will take a little while to find your perfect pre game meal but believe me, it will be well worth the trial and error. One important note: do not base your pre-game meal on how well you hit or performed. You might be full of energy and totally focused all game but go 0-4 with 4 solid line drives.

Post-Game Meals

Post-game meals are all about recovery. The quicker you get a good balanced meal in after a game the better it is for you because you will be helping your body recover quicker and in time for your next workout, practice or game so consume that post-game meal as soon as you can—no longer than 1-2 hours post game.

Your post-game meal should be similar to your pre-game meal. You need the balance of all of your macronutrients all the time. Here is an example of a good whole food post-game meal:

- Steak 6-8 ounces grilled

- Baked potato with butter

- Baby spinach salad with strawberries, walnuts, goat cheese, oil and vinegar

This meal will replace lost carbohydrate stores and give you enough protein for muscle repair and a good supply of healthy fats for nervous system repair.

Hydration

It is important to make sure you are properly hydrated at all times, not just before, during, or after a game. Once dehydrated it can take up to 24 hours to rehydrate. Studies show that if your body is dehydrated only 1%, you will lose 10% of muscle contractile strength. If you get dehydrated during a hot summer game, you can drink all the water you want in the dugout but it's going to take a long time for it to get where your body needs it. Your strength, power, and energy will not be operating at 100%. Keep hydrated all the time!

How much water do I need?

You should strive to drink half of your body weight in ounces of water daily. This will keep you properly hydrated. For example, if you weigh 180 lbs. you would need 90 ounces of water per day and more on extremely hot days where you are sweating profusely. The best water to drink during hot summer games (providing you have been staying hydrated all day long) is spring water with a pinch of sea salt in it. The sea salt will help maintain your mineral balance during the game.

High carbohydrate drinks such as Gatorade might have added minerals in them but the high sugar content will cause an energy crash later in the game. Remember whole foods? Water has one ingredient and if you add natural sea salt it's better than something with added sugar, food dyes, and chemicals and it won't cause a sugar crash. Drink plenty of water before, during, and after the game.

My tip on Hydration:

When you wake up, drink 16 oz. of water! Immediately. It's best to re-hydrate yourself after lack of hydration while you're sleeping. This 'life hack' is something I do every day; I believe it helps me get a great start to my day.

Twitter: @mdfitcon Instagram: @mikeduffyspersonaltraining

Transitions

Youth ➜ HS

Throughout my youth, my life revolved around baseball. Baseball, baseball, and more baseball. Hitting lessons, fielding lessons, pitching lessons—all of it. I had a batting cage in my backyard and I even had a real pitching mound installed into the ground so that I could throw bullpens to my Dad or my pitching coach at the time. From little league up until about 7th grade, I was very overweight (as you can see in those two pictures). I wish I had played multiple sports as a youth, so I could've increased my athleticism, which would've helped my weight problem, sure, but would've assisted me to perform even better on the field. My weight, which was one of my darkest insecurities at the time, made me realize that I needed to start working out and eating right. This is when I started to train hard. I was working out with Tom Kalieta, my athletic trainer all through high school. I owe it to my parents for giving me the opportunity to better myself and lose weight. I owe it to Tom, for instilling a hard work ethic in me at such a young age and for providing me with the guidance I needed to get myself in better shape. I also owe it to myself, for putting in the work and taking my development seriously before I entered high school baseball. When high school came around, I started to grow, lean out, and I was well-equipped with improved athleticism.

The youth baseball to high school baseball transition is such an amazing thing. It's great because this is the first time a kid may be away from parents. This transition is crucial because it's ultimately the first time a kid has the option and opportunity to develop on his/her own. Quick note to parents: when your son/daughter enters high school sports... coaches don't really care about you anymore. They expect your children to talk for themselves. Looking back, I loved this transition because it was the first time that I would practice without having my dad in my ear. It was the only time I could practice and develop as a player myself. This transition is extremely important for another reason. Around these ages, you see that your body starts to change and develop. The game changes. As a freshman in high school, you are most certainly not the big dog you may have been in middle school. High school sports are incredibly competitive and you have to prepare for that. On the high school level, youths also have to adapt to the new practice/game schedule. They have to get used to practicing and playing 5-6 days of the week.

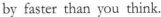

HS ➔ College

In this chapter, you'll read about many college players' experiences on their transition from playing at the high school level to the college level.

MY TRANSITION

What to Expect Going into College

If there's one thing I learned in my short college baseball experience, it's that the season flies. Time goes by faster than you think. As easy as it may be getting caught up with all of the practices, all of the workouts, and all of the games, it's important to take a step back and really soak in the moments you encounter on a daily basis. Ever since I've hung up my cleats, I miss the feeling of smelling the cut grass, picking up a pearly white, and just tossing it around to one of my best friends. I miss the sound of the sizzle the ball used to make when my throwing partner threw it to me. I miss the sound of a ball hitting my glove perfectly in the pocket. I miss putting 'two in the pink' and playing 'two ball' before a game. These small memories of the game are what I miss the most. For most people, college baseball is the highest level they'll reach and when their

time is due, they'll feel the same exact feeling I feel right now. When you know, you know.

From a physical standpoint, college baseball is a lot different than high school baseball. The game is played at a faster pace over a longer duration of time. You're no longer playing with kids that are the same age as you, but you're playing with kids who are grown men. In college baseball, you have very little room for error. In high school, the defense could make a ton of errors but it wouldn't matter. You can easily scratch those mistakes with a high scoring offensive inning. Those high-scoring innings, those innings where the offense never gets out— where the defense is literally handing you runs— are very rare at the collegiate level. Each out counts. Each pitch counts. The weight room matters. Sleep matters. Especially in college, when you're on this very strict schedule, you have to find a way to manage your time: do homework, study, workout, practice more, and get quality sleep.

The college baseball schedule is different. For us, at Montclair State, we would have class that would have to end around 11am-12pm. If we didn't have a game, we had a practice. The NCAA grants a specific amount of practice days in a week. These amount of hours/days vary from DI-DIII levels. Coaches will push you up until that NCAA limit regardless, and will probably find a loophole or two around these limitations. It's not like high school, where it may rain, outside practice gets cancelled, and then there's no practice. College coaches make sure practice gets accomplished, no matter what the circumstances may be.

That's one of the things I had to grow up with: Northeast weather. The beginning of the spring would suck. It'd be 30 degrees out and we were practicing outside, or it'd be raining/snowing so we'd have to practice in our gymnasium or at an inside facility for 5 days of the week. I envy players that live down south, who can practice and train outside all year long.

Master Time Management

My advice to high school players is to master time management. The ability to plan out your day, figure out what you need to do and when you need to do it, is crucial. As a regular college student, it's easy to procrastinate. Non-student athletes (a little biased) have all of the time in the world to go to classes, maybe workout, and get school work done. College baseball players don't have that luxury, so, time management is something that you should get acquainted with fast.

Lastly, if you do get the privilege to play college baseball, or even professionally, cherish every single moment. There will come a time when you are no longer lacing your cleats or strapping your batting gloves. Enjoy it.

Andrea Dalatri Old Dominion University IF

Photography Courtesy of CB Wilkins

"Freshman year of college is without a doubt one of the most memorable years of a person's life. An 18-year-old kid is forced to transition from living at home to living in a totally new place, making new friends, learning a new lifestyle, balancing sports and academics, and so much more. Although it seems like a handful, it really turns into some of the most fun a kid can have. Throughout my experience so far, a few things that helped keep me on track were having balance in my day, treating my body right, and learning from older teammates around me.

In order to have a successful day and to not let small stressful moments turn into bigger problems, it is important to balance out your day. When I say that, it means to make time for school, sports, and friends every day. I found this to be vital to my mental stability because it gave me time each day to enjoy what college is all about.

Another very important lesson I learned was how crucial it is to treat your body right. Right off the bat, the new freshmen are exposed to an incredible volume of working out and on field practice that wear and tear a person's body over time. If not treated correctly, this can lead to an injury in the long run. For this reason, it is imperative to take advantage of the resources around you. It's up to you to go to the trainer's room to get treatment or stretch out, take ice baths, do soft tissue work, or whatever else you need at the time. You never want stuff done in the weight room or practice to limit your full potential when it comes time for games or scrimmages when it is time to prove yourself.

Finally, listening and absorbing information from those around you is always important. They've been there, they've done it, and they know what it takes to stay healthy and compete at a high level. To get a head start on these things, it **never hurts to ask questions** and learn as much as possible."

"The Game Doesn't Owe You Anything."

Sal Monticciolo- La Salle University IF

"In high school, I was always pretty good because naturally, I was a big kid. The game came quick to me. I remember being nervous about playing at the collegiate level because it's really that next phase. You're walking onto a new team, where you're back to that 'freshman' role which is something that you live out of once and then you go back to it a second time. It brings back a lot of obstacles. You're no longer this big dog you were in high school. The biggest thing I had to adapt to in college was just putting in the work. No questions asked. The game doesn't owe you anything.

Ty Dudley- Oklahoma Christian University RHP

"The transition from high school baseball to college baseball can be summed up by saying that it is a variety of emotions. This time in your baseball career will be an event that will shape the way you think and play baseball for the rest of your time between the lines. This transition will put you to the test physically and mentally. The college venture is a whole new aspect to what you have experienced in high school. With that being said, this journey will also help your love for the game grow due to being a part of something bigger than yourself and coming together as a group of guys from all over the country to achieve a common goal.

Commonly, as a freshman you are expected to pay your dues to the team and use your first year to better yourself so you can truly help the team in the coming years. Acknowledgement and acceptance of this expectation is a very important part of starting your collegiate career. At this moment in time, you get to choose what kind of player you want to be going forward— a fresh start in some sense. You can choose if you want to just have fun while going to college, or you can take advantage of getting an education while having the privilege to play your sport for an organization that wants you to be there.

A common feeling upon entering the collegiate league is intimidation. The competition you will face from other colleges, as well as in your own locker room is intense. You may come into college at 18 years old while some of the seniors may be 22 or 23 and might possibly be competing for the same position. You realize that you are no longer the high school superstar but now are just one of the many high school superstars. This should make you aware that you need to work harder, longer, and smarter to earn a coveted starting position. Additionally, the opposing lineups are loaded with good hitters and the rotation is stacked with elite pitchers. Often you won't be able to tell the top of the lineup from the bottom. At this level, everything you do 24/7, affects your playing time— your study habits so you remain eligible, your workout habits so you get stronger, and your coachability so you continue to learn the game— all play a part in your success. These attributes will take you far in baseball as well as in life. Work hard and enjoy the journey!"

Jack Harnisch- Fordham University IF

"For me, the biggest transition from high school to college baseball was the intensity and speed of the game. Every runner is faster, every pitcher throws harder and has better off-speed, and the ground balls are hit faster. I think the biggest thing that I struggled with— and I think many players from high school to college do as well— is failure. In high school, hitting is much easier. Simply because on a week to week basis, you do not face as many quality arms, and the breaking balls you see are not as sharp. At least for me, I was used to just sitting fastball and swinging as hard as I could and attacking every at bat. Most days, in 3 or 4 at bats, I could just get up there and barrel up a few fastballs by just being overaggressive. In college, that does not work.

My first at bat of college baseball came at Texas A&M, pinch hitting in the 6th inning down by a few runs against a freshman coming out of the bullpen. I stepped in the box and kept in mind that he was probably one of their lower tier guys out of the bullpen. The first pitch was 95 MPH on the scoreboard, as it showed on the scoreboard in the outfield. I was late and fouled it off. The next pitch was another fastball, again coming in mid-90's and with adrenaline, seemed like 100; I got beat a little and hit a high pop up to center field. As the season went on, I began to realize the major difference in college baseball: accepting failure. You can be as prepared as possible, focused, ready to play, make good swings, and still get beat and go 0 for 4. You could be in perfect position and make an error because a ball was hit on the screws and took a crazy hop. So, in that way, I would also say that that is the advice (although only being 1 year in) I would give to someone about to be a freshman in DI baseball. You have to understand everyone is going to be good— pitchers, hitters, and fielders. You could hit a bomb that would be a home run and you're the hero at your high school field, but in college, the center fielder is camped under it. You could smoke a ball in the hole and a great DI infielder makes a diving play.

College baseball is just a more difficult game in all facets, and that is something you need to understand before you enter the collegiate level. It is not high school anymore, and the mental game is even more important. How do you respond to a 0 for 4 day or even a 0 for 11 streak? A tough error, or a ball you hit hard in the gap and they made a diving play? The college game is more about your attitude and preparation, and you are not good enough to just go out there and "wing" it and be better than everyone like you may have been able to do in high school. You are going to fail, and it is all about whether you understand that and how you respond to it. I believe that is what separates the decent college baseball players from the great ones, even though everyone was *great* in high school."

Joe Colucci- Emerson College IF

"Growing up, I was never the most talented kid. I was smaller, less athletic, and not particularly strong or fast at all. However, I looked at this as a blessing in disguise. I learned at an early age how to work hard and do what it takes to improve at the hardest game in the world. When I did develop physically, I was better for it having that knowledge.

That made the transition from high school ball to college much more seamless in my opinion.

The biggest difference in my opinion is simply how much is expected of you both in terms of time commitment and on field matters. Practices/workouts are longer and occur more often, sometimes even overlapping lifts and practices on the same day. When you initially participate in practices and games, there are certain aspects of the game that you are simply expected to understand upon arrival. There is very little teaching going on at this level. These coaches do not have time to teach you how to hit, field, and throw. This is not to say that they won't make adjustments with you to get the best out of you, but, their main focus is the team as a whole and ensuring team success, not developing individual players. College coaches expect you to be accountable and mature. They expect you to represent their program with some respect. Keep in mind: no helmet throwing, no yelling at umpires, and respect the game and your teammates.

For me, personally, the biggest aspect of my training that changed was my lifting and nutrition. Since I was a small kid graduating high school (165lbs), it was important for me to put on some size and strength to compete at this new level. Today, at about 190-195lbs, the ball comes off my bat differently. My arm strength has improved and even weighing in 30lbs heavier, my 60 time has gone down from 7.3 in high school to 6.86 (personal best). I attribute this to my time lifting. Use that time and space to make yourself the best athlete you can be. I'd advise all young ball players that want to make it to the next level that they can and should be getting in the weight room sooner than they think."

JUCO

In this chapter, you'll learn a bit about the JUCO life and what this route entails.

Dan Drullinger- Pitching Coach - Cerro Coso Community College

"Junior college baseball is a fantastic world, full of talent, camaraderie, and opportunity. The perceptions and reality of it being a "last resort" are rightfully fading into the past. In my opinion, junior college baseball is such a pure form of the sport -- guys coming together as one unit to play for the love of the game. Yes, it is hard work, as it is at any level, but it is also downright fun. Sure, there is an individual element to playing in junior college yet the relationships built and bonds formed that come from the proverbial grind of junior college are special.

Despite the obvious differences between a junior college and a four-year institution, I think the gap between the two is smaller than many may think. While junior colleges may not have the budgets a four-year might, the resources a lot of junior colleges make available to their athletes are excellent—from tools and technology to facilities and personnel. The name of the game in junior college baseball is development, and many junior colleges work hard to shorten the learning curve in order to prepare athletes to succeed at the next level, both on the field and in the classroom.

Playing junior college baseball is a bet you place on yourself. A bet that with hard work, dedication, and the necessary reps, you can achieve an opportunity to play at the highest level your skillset and mindset will allow. So much growth can happen in the span of two years that opportunities that may seem unrealistic now — like earning a four-year scholarship to your dream school or getting drafted to play professionally — may not seem so far-fetched at the end of those two years. The best part of junior college is knowing that for most, it is a step in the journey and not the final destination. It's an opportunity to better prepare yourself to play at the highest level. When four-year coaches recruit a junior college player, it's oftentimes because they need a guy to step in and compete right away. They know these players have been battle-tested at a high level and can likely make an impact for the program immediately. Take a look at your favorite college baseball team's roster and note how many guys got there via junior college; the number may surprise you.

For those who are unsure of the idea of going the junior college route, I'd recommend approaching the process with clear eyes and an open mind. Work to understand the program, the college and its academic offerings, the coaching staff and how they approach development, and the program's track record of moving their athletes to the next level. Pair what you learn with the goals you have set for yourself both athletically and academically and you may find the junior college route is the best fit for you right now."

Twitter: @DanDrullinger Instagram: @rolliedingers

Mikey Wynne- Brookdale Community College RHP

"The Junior College Route is unique in ways that majority of the baseball community knows but also in ways that people don't get to see. I attended Brookdale CC in Lincroft, New Jersey. For me, this school was only about 25 minutes from my house so I commuted every day, as did the majority of the team. Some kids who lived out of state or far away lived in a house in the area. The reason I chose to go JUCO is because of the two reasons that most people choose this route. I didn't have interest from schools I wanted to go to and I did not know what I wanted to study. I chose Brookdale because it is my county's Community College so the price of school was very affordable. So, it seems that the best way to get two years of education while saving money would be this route. I think a lot of people shy away from this route because of the label it holds. I know when I was younger, I was trying to avoid going to a community college as much as possible. But when you look at the numbers and the benefits it has, it was an easy choice. A lot of people don't like the fact of staying home and the sense that you're not really at college, which I get, I felt the same way for the first few months. Then, I started to realize the positives of it. I was able to maintain training with my trainer (Shout-out Tom), eat good meals every night, and if I wanted to, I was able to work and make some extra cash here and there.

Now, the story of Junior College baseball is something that cannot be compared to anything, literally. Whether it be the bus rides, after game meals, or everyday life, it was one of a kind. I'll start with the struggles... our field. Having to maintain your own field was something none of us liked but also something that came with the JUCO route. Everything we did was incomparable to a Division 1 school, but that's the beauty of it. It brought all of the guys together because we were all in it for the same reasons. There is something about 18-hour bus rides down to Florida every spring break that really connect us as a family and rooming with kids that will become your closest friends but initially come off as complete strangers. There is something about playing 15 games in a week that creates a unique bond between the players. JUCO is so unique in ways that it doesn't sound fun or appealing. When put into these special situations, there is nothing else to do other than **having fun**. It creates an atmosphere that none of us are used to, but one that puts school and baseball into perspective. None of us were playing for the names on the back, but we all played for the name on the front of the jersey, essentially putting Lincroft, New Jersey on a bigger scale within the baseball community. Before making the decision to come here, I didn't expect anything to be how it was and I think that is how people see JUCO in general: you don't really know what to expect. There is beauty behind the outlook. We weren't going to get the free clothes and all that nice stuff but we were there to play baseball. Both of my two years we were continuously ranked nationally in the top 10 in the nation for Division 3 JUCO. We competed with top teams in the country, and that is why we chose this route— to play at the highest level we can. The fancy facilities and clothes are nice but at the end of the day, we are all playing the same game. All in all, JUCO is one of a kind and gets a negative outlook because of its label, but it was the greatest experience of my life."

College ➔ MiLB

In this chapter, you'll read about a few professional players' experiences on their transition from playing at the college level to the professional level (MiLB).

Sam McMillan- Catcher in the Detroit Tigers Organization

"I was drafted in the fifth round out of high school in 2017, and chose to forgo a scholarship to the University of Florida to head straight to the minor leagues. Whenever I'm back home in the offseason there are two main questions I get from friends and family curious about what it's like and how things are going. "What's it like going straight from high school to pro ball?" and "If you could go back, would you still sign out of high school or would you decide to go to college?" I'll try to answer both of these questions in the most non-biased way I can.

Let's start with the transition from high school to pro ball. I played at Suwannee High School in Live Oak, FL and for the Florida Burn travel team out of Sarasota, FL in the summers and falls of my junior and senior years. My high school was a 5A school (out of 8 divisions, 8A being the highest) and played a fairly hard schedule my senior year. We probably faced around 5-8 future Division 1 arms that year out of 25 games, so as far as high school baseball goes, we faced some really good competition. My travel team (the Burn) played in all of the big Perfect Game tournaments you find most teams at and went fairly deep into the playoffs in a lot of them, so before I had been drafted I had already seen a lot of players play that would go on to be high draft picks and college stars and eventually some of them would reach the big leagues. Even though I had been fortunate to have already played against a lot of the best players in my class, minor league baseball was still a little bit of a culture shock (I'd say most guys in my position would say the same). Nothing you do in HS is going to be much like having to go out and play nearly every day in an environment you're not used to, against players older and more talented than what you're used to. The best advice I can give to any player making a big jump in competition is **not to panic**. One of the biggest things it takes in the game of baseball is confidence, and sometimes you need to rely on the ability to be confident in yourself when not many other people would be.

Very few players get drafted into the MiLB and have ridiculous success all the way up into the big leagues. You're going to take some lumps along the way, and how you react to those failures defines a lot of guy's careers. I feel like I've made a lot of growth my three years in the minor leagues so far. I've learned to deal with bad games, weeks, months, and even seasons. Even though I'm not in the big leagues yet (and who knows if I ever will be or not), my experience so far has shown me the mental and physical toughness that it takes to make a living in the game. It is by no means for the faint of heart, but I don't say that to make it sound like it's not fun anymore or so hard that you shouldn't do everything you can to put yourself in that place. I've had some of the best times of my life in the minor leagues. I've also been tested like I never have before, and I'm proud of that. At the end of the day I'm working as hard as I can towards a dream I've had since the first time I picked up a ball—whether or not I realize that dream. As long as I know that I gave every ounce of effort I had, I can live with whatever outcome I get out of that. That's all you can really ask for. The game doesn't owe me anything. Now, I go out and prepare and play with the mindset that nothing is going to get handed to me. Anything I achieve from now will be directly because of the work that I and the people put around me to help me have put in. That's the biggest take away I hope any young players reading this realize that your natural ability is only going to take you so far in life.

It's the guys that focus all their time and energy into making it happen that are the guys that get what they want out of the game. There is no substitute for that. Now the second question I get asked a lot, "Would you change your decision to skip college if you could? It's worth noting that 2020 would've been my junior season in college and the first year I would've been eligible for the draft. Due to the coronavirus epidemic, this year's college season was shortened drastically and it looks like the draft will be as well. If I had known that, I DEFINITELY would've signed out of high school, but obviously I had no way of knowing that at the time.

Even if things had gone completely normal, I still believe that I made the right decision for myself. A lot of factors go into people's decision on the draft or college out of high school. Ultimately, you only get one chance to be a college baseball player and once you turn that down there is no going back. I was fortunate enough to have signed to my dream college since day one, and I don't doubt that playing there would've been an unreal experience. Once I started weighing out my options, I felt that pro ball was a better fit for me personally (although it's worth noting a lot of my teammates I talk to are glad that they went to college and didn't sign out of high school).

For me, the main reasons for signing were that if I played to the best of my potential I could find myself knocking on the door to the big leagues a lot faster than if I went to college, and if I didn't play well or got injured I would still have a signing bonus that was a lot more than what I ever dreamed I'd get out of baseball. I also felt that missing out on a great college experience was a price I was willing to pay for the chance to chase a lifelong dream of mine. Another thing I think gets looked over a lot is the ability to take care of school even while you're playing in pro ball. One of the scariest things for me was potentially being out of the game at some point with no college degree and having to either find a career where I didn't need one or having to go back to school as a washed-up minor leaguer.

It turns out that if you want to you can really chip away at some school while you're still playing. Most guys drafted out of high school get college scholarship plans thrown into their contracts. This is an extra sum of money that is there for you if you want to go back to school. It can only be used for tuition, books, renting an apartment during your classes, etc. It's not like it's money that actually goes in your pocket, but it's nice to know that all of that is basically taken care of (aside from the fact that the money gets taxed like income, so you do have to pay for it but it's only a fraction of what it would normally cost). So, using that I've been able to take care of a few online college classes while playing. I usually take one or two classes each fall and spring. It overlaps with the end of the season and some of spring training but it's not too much to handle when you're talking about just doing a little bit here and there a couple days a week. Plus, it's a way to get an offseason apartment at a big discount if you're from a small town like me and don't want to live at home where resources to train are minimal. That's just one thing I found out later that would've played a bigger role in my decision if I had known sooner. At the end of the day, there really isn't a wrong choice. I felt incredibly lucky to be in the spot I was. Who knows, if I had gone to college, I might be sitting here saying that I'm glad that I went to college. There are a lot of ways to get to the big leagues and no matter what, the cream will eventually get to the top, I suppose."

Brandon Martorano- Catcher in the San Francisco Giants Organization

"Consistency is the one common denominator you will find in every major league player."

"My transition from college to pro ball is more of a mental transition than anything physical. In college, especially at a place like North Carolina, everything in your daily life is extremely structured. From class to practice to meals to tutoring, all of your daily tasks are emailed to you the night before every day. There is not much autonomy when it comes to college baseball. I don't say that as a slight, it really is just the nature of the beast. In college, the ONLY emphasis is winning ball games. Each member of the team practices, goes to class/tutors, lifts, eats, breathes in order to better the team. In college, you have to tailor your game to best fit the needs of the team and what the team needs to win a ball game on any given day. Pro ball is far from that, especially in the minor leagues. While there is still some emphasis on winning, the main goal as a player in the minor leagues is to constantly improve your game and sharpen your skills in order to give yourself an opportunity to play in the big leagues. The minor

245

leagues, therefore, are inherently selfish whereas college ball is 100% team oriented. I found, in my short experience so far (thanks COVID-19) that pro ball is very liberating. Playing professional baseball has afforded me the opportunity to really become self-sufficient. You are thrust into a situation where the future of your career solely depends on your own desire to improve your game every day. Yes, there are coaches, coordinators, and veteran players there to help and guide me, but at the end of the day, my career will ultimately be what I make of it myself.

With that being said, I definitely have trained differently than when I was in college. Now whenever I say that people always wonder what different PHYSICAL things I may have done to better my game. And while yes, I have made some small minor tweaks physically, I feel as if I have benefited more from training the mental side of things rather than physical. This is the polar opposite of how I went about things in college. In college I was always focused on physical tweaks that I could make to help myself obtain success. In pro ball, I shifted my focus to more mental strength training. Focusing on trusting in my ability, addressing and handling failure and developing a steady routine to follow that works for me are the three main things I really focused on improving when I got to professional baseball.

A baseball season is a marathon, not a sprint. The minor leagues will inherently bring a myriad of challenges to EVERY player, regardless of how talented that player is. The people that you see on television are those who are able to control the mental side of their game the best. They are able to handle failure exceptionally well, never get too high or too low, and above all: stay CONSISTENT. Consistency is the one common denominator you will find in every major league player. Therefore, I would say the biggest thing I have changed from college to pro ball is to figure out how to be consistent."

Andre Nnebe- Outfielder in the Milwaukee Brewers Organization

"For me, college was great just to develop as an all-around person, meet many great lifelong friends, and improve as a player. I spent a lot of time injured in college, so I'd say my experience of college baseball was full of more downs than ups but I think the discipline and structure of college baseball and academics helped me to develop and transition well into pro baseball.

Once I got into pro baseball, I'd say the environment is more relaxed and coaches are there more to develop players, as opposed to just trying to win games. I definitely miss the hyper competitive aspect of college baseball and the dugout energy. If you really take advantage of all the resources in pro baseball, you expedite your maturity as a player because you are playing games every day and facing better competition.

I think that college has a lot more structure, which is good for guys coming from high school. Six AM lifts, team meetings, etc. are not always fun but they give you a good foundation for the next level. Once you get to the pros, there's a lot of equipment and resources available, but it's more up to you to make the most of it. You also have a little more freedom during the offseason in where you train, so you can have a more individualized plan. I spent this last offseason at Sparta Science in Menlo Park, CA. They train all types of high-level athletes, and use force plates to gather data and customize workout plans for each individual based on how they move.

The minor league schedule is pretty much baseball from 1-10pm. Travel is pretty much all by bus, and guys don't really make a whole lot of money until they make it to the big leagues. The schedule is fairly similar to a college baseball schedule for game days, just more games per week."

MLB

This section contains former 14-year MLB Veteran, Pete Harnisch touching base on some of the main topics discussed throughout the entirety of this book. Harnisch compiled a career record of 111-103 and an ERA of 3.89.

Pete Harnisch- Former 14 Year MLB Veteran

Pete and Jack (son) at Yankee Stadium

Pete answered the following questions for me:
1. How has the game changed since you've played?

2. How did you respond to adversity?

3. What advice can you give younger guys who want to achieve their dream in professional baseball?

The game has changed a ton since my days. Stats such as on base percentage (OBP), WAR, FIP, and others are looked at through a different lens and mean way more now as the game has **become way more analytical**. Playing for one run offensively is a thing of the past. Hitters have a totally different approach; 2 strike approaches seem to be a thing of the past.

I dealt with adversity by learning to continue to compete and grind (fight) no matter what. Every single inning, game, and time that I took the ball, I was always **competing**. I always looked at the next opportunity to get an out and do my best in any situation to keep my team in the game.

My advice to young pitchers is simple.

1. Work hard.

2. Always be a great teammate.

3. Get a routine and stick to it. (See "Keys to Success")

4. Compete and fight every single pitch and every time you take the ball from *start* to *finish*, no matter what happens.

5. Always be prepared in any way possible.

Most importantly, learn to **listen** and **ask questions**. You never know who may teach you something and truly listening and hearing any and all advice can often lead you to something that may help more than you could imagine.

Keys to Success

This chapter is full of general advice to players who want to really step up their game. The importance of 'always learning', proper routine scheduling, and other insights/advice from many players and coaches make up the entirety of this chapter. Find something that resonates with you!

LEARNING

My advice for anyone reading is this: Always keep learning. Strive to know more. Strive to apply your knowledge more. Strive to understand your body, your strengths, and your weaknesses. This statement is not meant for only baseball players. It's a statement for life. It doesn't matter what sport you play or what profession you work in.

Studying psychology in school has taught me that the brain can change—the brain evolves. Through neuroplasticity, our neurons make all sorts of new connections when we learn and acquire new information. These connections are also made when we experience certain things and other stimuli. Contrary to many beliefs, our knowledge and our brain structure are not fixed. Our brain can actually be rewired physically! Through learning, our brain can grow. By re-shaping the way we think (Cognitive Behavioral Therapy) and mindfulness training, people can change their lives in a more positive way. For athletes, this could assist your playing career tremendously.

Without diving into the complexity of psychology in more depth, the main point is this: **learn**. I suggest **reading**. Reading is incredibly neglected nowadays, living in this generation. I thought so too. I've read maybe 1 book in my 4 years of HS. Keep in mind that I was "required" to do summer reading each year. Reading is a form of meditation for me. It calms my mind and weirdly enough, I've grown an obsession to learn through reading as much as I can. With that being said, I know many people despise reading, or they may struggle with it. That's fine, too. As we may live in a generation with limited readers, we also live in a time where nearly everything is available online on the Internet. Information and resources are certainly available.

For the Internet Learner

Watch videos on YouTube. Watch documentaries. Watch interviews. Listen to podcasts! We all have access to these resources for free! If you want to be the best baseball player you can be, you must be obsessed with learning. Learn from the best. We are blessed with watching the best baseball players to ever play. Want to become a better hitter? Watch Mike Trout. What is he doing that you're not? How does he prepare himself?

What types of foods does he put into his body? How much sleep does he get? What's his workout regimen like? How many swings a day does he take? If you meet your favorite player at a spring training game, your first reaction shouldn't be, "Oh, let me get an autograph." It should be, "How can I do what you do?" There's a method to all of the success you see on the field. There's always a story behind it. We just don't see that other side.

REACHING — HOME PLATE

BE A STUDENT OF THE GAME

The **bolded** text are all of the books I have read this year. The other books are those I plan on reading sometime in the near future.

I order my books from Thriftbooks or Amazon.

If you recommend any books, please send them my way!

MY BOOKLIST (short list... full list @ (www.reachinghomeplate.com)

- ➤ **The Mental Game of Baseball**: H.A Dorfman

- ➤ **Presence**: Amy Cuddy

- ➤ Daily Stoic: Ryan Holiday

- ➤ Power Sleep: James B. Maas

- ➤ **Mamba Mentality**: Kobe Bryant

- ➤ **Above the Line**: Urban Meyer

- ➤ **Jeter Unfiltered**: Derek Jeter

- ➤ **Mindset**: Carol Dweck

- ➤ Relentless: Tim Grover

- ➤ **Life is Yours to Win**: Augie Garrido

- ➤ **It Takes What It Takes**: Trevor Moawad

- ➤ **Man's Search for Meaning**: Victor Frankl

- ➤ **Heads up Baseball**: Ken Ravizza and Tom Hanson

- ➤ John Wooden on Leadership

- ➤ **Mind Gym**: Gary Mack

- ➤ **Legacy**: James Kerr

- ➤ **Talent is Never Enough**: John C. Maxwell

- ➤ Can't Hurt Me: Master Your Mind and Defying the Odds: David Goggins

KNOWLEDGE + APPLICATION =

IF YOU DO NOT LEARN, TAKE AN IDEA OR A LESSON FROM A BOOK, OR DO NOT APPLY THE KNOWLEDGE YOU ACQUIRED FROM IT, THE BOOK DOES YOU NO GOOD.

HAVING A GOOD ROUTINE

> "We are what we
> repeatedly do."
> - Aristotle

Humans are habitual creatures. We do the same unconscious things every single morning from when we wake up to when we go to bed. Life is always throwing curveballs at us– random hardship and conflict are always coming our way. If it's not one thing, it's another. We know this. Those curveballs, however, we can't control. What we can control though is the ability to develop good habits and establish a solid routine that starts our day off right and caps the night off.

"We are what we repeatedly do." – Aristotle. If we want to be the best baseball player we want to be, we need to prepare like one. It's important to take the necessary actions **every single day**.

I'm going to attach a small clip; In my freshman year of college, I gave a speech on why you should establish a good routine. Below is a video of my freshman roommate, teammate, and lifelong friend, Nick Cassano. Nick is one of the most dedicated people I know, however, all of our college friends thought he was crazy.

<u>Nick's AM Routine (YouTube Channel)</u>

Nick's Routine in College

- ➤ 5:30 - 5:45 AM ⇒ Snooze once @5:30, get up at 5:45

- ➤ 5:58 AM- At the gym (Gym opened at 6)

- ➤ 6- 7:15 AM- Workout

- ➤ 7:20 AM- Perry wakes up due to Nicky's Diner

- ➤ Breakfast- ⅔ cup of Oatmeal, 1 Stevia packet, 1 TBSP PB + 4 Egg Whites, ¼ cup of fat-free cheddar cheese and dabble of Frank's Red-Hot Sauce. Tall Glass of water. Two Multivitamins. 1 Acutane Pill.

- ➤ 7:40 AM- Shower ⇒ Dressed and ready by 8:05 AM

- ➤ 8:30- 12:45 PM- classes

- ➤ 1 - 3 PM ⇒ Practice

- ➤ 3 - 4 PM ⇒ Team Lift

- ➤ 4:30- 5 PM ⇒ Dinner @ Dining Hall

- ➤ 5:30- 10:00 Shower/ Nap/ Homework/ Facetime Girlfriend

- ➤ 10:30/11:00 Go to bed

EVERY DAY. Repeat. Repeat. Repeat.

Disclaimer: This is not suggesting you should wake up every morning at 5:30 in the morning. For Nick, this was an optimal time for him. It's important to discover what time(s) you operate the most efficient.

Why Having a Daily Routine is Important?

1. Good habits

2. Increases efficiency

3. No need for motivation

A good routine is the foundation of preparation. Being prepared, physically or mentally, is paramount for success. I'm no longer a college baseball player. If I could do it over again, I would prioritize my AM/PM routines. Attached are my *current* AM/PM routines, along with an example of how I schedule my days. My schedule is an example of something I got from Brian Cain, a mental performance coach. He called it the '168 plan'. There are 168 hours in a week and he has a great template on how his high-level athletes should schedule their week.

I was never an advocate for making my bed. I hated it. My thought process used to be: Why make my bed if I'm just going to hop back in it tonight? Anyone else think like this? Well, push that thought process out of your head because making your bed every morning is something so small, but has such a powerful impact on your day. Read the quote and watch the video (YouTube) from Retired Navy Seal William H. McCraven.

"If you make your bed every morning,
you will have accomplished the first
task of the day," he said. "It will give
you a small sense of pride, and it will
encourage you to do another task, and
another, and another. And by the end
of the day that one task completed
will have turned into many tasks
completed... if you can't do the little
things right, you'll never be able to do
the big things right. And if by chance
you have a miserable day, you will
come home to a bed that is made —
that you made."
**Retired U.S. Navy Admiral Seal
William H. McCraven**

EXAMPLE of my planned-out day

TUESDAY, FEBRUARY 4, 2020
7:45 am Wake Up
8:00- 8:15 Make bed, get ready
8:15-8:30 Success Hotline, Positive Affirmations
8:30-8:50 Drink a lot of water, Supplements + Breakfast
8:50-9:00 Drive and get coffee (Dunkin)
9:00-9:30 Drive to school for Classes
10:00-12:30 pm Classes- Experimental Psych
12:40-1:20 WorkoutQ1- Legs
1:20-1:50 Drive home
1:50-2:10 Lunch
2:10-2:30 SelfCare
2:30-3:30 HOMEWORK BLOCK
3:30-5:00 SelfCare- Read,
5:00-5:30 Dinner
5:30⇒ SelfCare + AM+PM ROUTINES + Meditation 5 min
10:00⇒ Sleep

AM ROUTINE

- ✓ Wake up
- ✓ **Make bed** + get ready
- ✓ Meditation 5 min
- ✓ Positive affirmations
- ✓ Foam roll. Stretch
- ✓ Brush Teeth, Breakfast
- ✓ Tackle the day

PM ROUTINE

- ✓ Shower, Brush Teeth
- ✓ Plan the next day out—outfits, books, schedule, tasks, etc.
- ✓ Read 30 min
- ✓ Meditation 5 min
- ✓ Sleep

Unfortunately, I did not schedule out my days when I played, however, I created an *example* schedule of what my day would have probably looked like:

7:00 AM Wake up
7:00-7:15 Make bed, Get ready
7:20-7:30 Drink a lot of water (32 oz.) Breakfast
7:35-8:00 Shower, Call Success Hotline, Positive Affirmations, *AM+PM ROUTINES*
8:05-8:15 Start walking to class, grab a coffee
8:30-11:15 Classes - Find time for a snack or two
11:30 Walk to Locker room
12:00 pm Prepare mentally for practice, Treatment? Packed Lunch? Snack?
1:00-4:00 Practice
4:15-5:00 Lift
5:10-5:30 Treatment
5:30-6:00 Dinner in Dining Hall- mingle with teammates/friends
6:05-6:15 SelfCare- Shower
6:20-7:00 HOMEWORK BLOCK
7:05-8:00 SelfCare- Xbox or more homework (if needed)
8:05-9:00 SelfCare- podcast? Visualization
9:05 *SelfCare* + *AM+PM ROUTINES* + Meditation 5 min
10:00⇒ Sleep

What's self-care? (Seen in my Example 168)

Self-care is essentially anything YOU need to get done to fulfill YOUR personal needs. It's imperative that you schedule at least one self-care block throughout your day, regardless of how busy you are. Allotting only 15 minutes of time to yourself is beneficial; it allows you to calm your occupied mind. Most dedicated athletes seem to overwork/over-exert themselves in order to reach their goals. It's OK to step back and relax, sometimes. Keep that in mind whenever you feel like you're drained or if you ever find yourself losing yourself in the process of achieving your aspirations. Routines can get monotonous and boring at times; however, self-care blocks provide you the opportunity to switch things up, without losing your ability to move forward with your day. DO NOT take advantage of this time you give yourself. DO NOT lose sight of the things you still need to accomplish. **Here's an example of my 'Self-Care' List. ATHLETES NEED SELF-CARE, TOO.**

- ✓ Xbox/Video games
- ✓ Reading
- ✓ Watching motivational videos/ Listen to Podcast
- ✓ Massage
- ✓ Phone calls w/ Family/Girlfriend
- ✓ Going out w/ Friends
- ✓ Haircut
- ✓ More sleep/power nap
- ✓ Hanging out with friends/family
- ✓ Getting/ Having a cup of Coffee
- ✓ Laying down in bed/ relaxing- Netflix/movie/ TV
- ✓ Laundry
- ✓ Going to stores- shopping, groceries, etc.
- ✓ DoorDashing- $$$
- ✓ Volunteering
- ✓ Any other type of errand

Sean Light CEO of 4A Health Former Strength Coach for Los Angeles Lakers & Arizona Diamondbacks

Directly from Sean's Blog:

Morning Routine: I think having a morning routine is really important. It seems like most really successful people have one. I really started trying to develop mine after reading *Tools of Titans* by Tim Ferriss. This is my routine:

- *4:30am:* Wake Up; Crush my 32oz Water; Brew Coffee
- 4:45am: Practice the Guitar
- 5:30am: Read
- 6:30am: Workout
- 7:30am: Get Hyper Focused
- 8:00am: Start Working

I tried all sorts of different things getting this started but this has been a routine that has been working for me for quite a while. More than anything else, I **believe morning routines get your day off on the right foot** and it sets you up for success for the rest of the day.

Focus: I don't think you should underestimate focus. I try to get all of my mental and physical energy going in the same direction towards the same goal. I have a goal of getting 3,500 webinar views this month and everything I do is geared towards making that happen. If I start also trying to start acquiring training clients, I am certainly going decrease my chances of hitting 3,500 views because I won't be giving that task/goal the same effort. I try to get my subconscious mind to be constantly turning in that direction, so that no matter what captures the attention of my conscious mind, I always snap back to what needs to be my focus.

Twitter: @Slight20 Instagram: @slight20

Their $0.02

Coach Trottier

Becoming Your Own Person

For any athlete who's trying to play in college or the professional level, there's a lot that can be said: "Get bigger and stronger" can be one thing, but that's low-hanging fruit. Everyone knows that. What's going to separate those from the game, or to find success wherever they go? They must become their own person. Don't try and be someone you're not. Become the best possible version of you. Own it. Know when to go, know when to stop, know when to hold yourself accountable. Don't be afraid to ask for help. Don't let the ego get the best of you.

Josh Tols

Live, Love, & Learn

Don't limit yourself! There are so many good programs out there. There are great NJCAA, DII, DIII and NAIA programs that will help you develop and get to the next level! The mentality of "DI or bust" is extremely close minded.

One thing that helped me progress through college to Indy ball then to Pro ball was a genuine love of the game and always having fun. It didn't matter where I was playing or what league I was in, I always tried to find a way to enjoy it, learn from it, and find a way to keep on moving.

Brad Case

There's Always Someone Better than You

I think the best advice I can give to anyone in really any part of life is knowing that there's always someone better than you out there. My whole life I grew up in New York, a place not exactly known for good youth baseball. Every time I threw a baseball, went on a run, worked out, etc. I told myself that there was someone out there born with more talent than I have now. There's a lot of guys I play with and play against that I know are just better than me. The only way I can beat them is if I work even harder than them.

Jake Lawrie

Love the Game & Love the Process

Do not play a sport if you do not love it. The idea that you are bound to play a sport just because you're deemed "good" at it is ridiculous. If you want to be about it, then embrace it. It is definitely not easy but you have to love the process and everything about it because it will only last so long.

Coach Victor Diaz

Discipline and Presence

Best advice for an athlete who aspires to play at the next level is: **stay disciplined and be present**. Those two things work hand in hand because to be present, you need to be disciplined. Everyone has goals and everyone has dreams but we have to be the best we can be where we are currently at. Invest your time in mastering where you currently are. Become a better person, son, friend, teammate, and player.

Andre Nnebe

Have a Love for the Game

I think the most important thing is a love for the game. I know so many kids who dominated in little league, but eventually lost interest in the sport. On the flip side, you see kids in high school and college who have average talent but their passion and work ethic can get them drafted and lead to longer success.

Also, I think that development is really important. A lot of kids go to showcases everywhere but don't take lifting and proper training seriously. Sometimes you have to look yourself in the mirror and realize your best bet to get recruited or drafted is to improve first, rather than just showcase.

Tommy Winterstein

Have No Regrets

Be able to look back when it is all said and done and have no regrets. To do that, in my opinion, you have to have that accountability to yourself to know you did everything in your power to put yourself in a position to succeed and that you worked to the best of your ability every day. If you do that, at the end of the day, you just let the chips fall where they may. You have to know you did everything in your power to put yourself in that position to be able to look back **with no regrets**.

Brandon Martorano

Have Self-Trust

As for some advice I would offer to someone with aspirations of playing professional baseball, I would say one thing: **trust in yourself**. Self-doubt kills more success and kills more careers than failure ever will. The individuals that are able to stay steady through all the trials and tribulations that come with the game of baseball are those that will be able to play the game for a long time. With that, I would also say it is nearly impossible to play this game at a high level without doing something to improve your skills every single day. Hard work is invaluable. Whether it is going to the gym, hitting off the tee, throwing long toss, or simply visualizing yourself having success, you cannot play this game at a high level without hard work. You certainly can try, but don't expect to find much success when doing so.

People have this preconceived notion that professional baseball players are where they are because they have been blessed with talent that the average little leaguer will never have. People in the baseball world look at big leaguers sometimes as super human. I fell into that same trap when I was a young kid. I immortalized players that I looked up to and always wondered what they had or did to get to their position that other people just don't have. While, yes, it is true you must possess a lot of talent to play this game at a high level, the reality is that if you are willing to simply work harder than everyone else, and take an extremely committed focus to bettering yourself as a player both physically and mentally every day, you will always put yourself in a position to succeed. Baseball does not promise you anything, so do everything you can every single day to shift the odds in your favor.

Nick Weisheipl- Head Baseball Coach @ Cabrini University

Biggest pieces of advice for *college athletes*:

If you are unsure of something, unhappy with something, or having second thoughts/are being persuaded to have second thoughts about your current program, speak with your coach about it. A large percentage of misunderstandings and misinformation are due to a lack of communication, clarity, or a product of mental gymnastics student-athletes do to legitimize their unhappiness. Pulling the trigger on transferring/exploring other options without first having a candid conversation with the head coach is reckless and of poor judgement.

Coach Croushore

"There is NO substitute for hard work."

Work harder than everyone else on your team— at your game, your conditioning, your strength program, your academics, and everything else. There is NO substitute for hard work. You do the work and your future will play out how it should. Lastly...believe in your dream...if you love this game and want to play at the next level, you better believe you can be there and produce at that level.

Tommy Eveld (Pitchers)

Keep it Simple

Success is something that is unexplainable. Sometimes you can make the best pitch in the best location and the scouting report will say that a guy can't hit a certain pitch and then he crushes it. Sometimes you will throw a guy a pitch that should get crushed and they swing and miss, get out, or don't swing at all. **I have found that when I am having success I am not overthinking on the mound.** When I'm struggling, I am thinking a lot on the mound. My advice is to keep it simple in the game. I do all of my drill work and heavy thinking before the game so that I can try to go out and pitch care free.

When I first started pitching professionally in 2016, I did not have checkpoints in my delivery. If I threw a bad pitch, I did not think about what I needed to do mechanically to fix it, I could just feel what was wrong and throw it better next time. It wasn't until 2019 in AAA that I started messing around with mechanical changes that I did not feel comfortable with. My delivery felt awkward and I was feeling for something on every throw. I was throwing too much in the pre-game throwing program and then throwing another 20-30 pitches in the bullpen before I would go in the game. I had nothing to fall back on because I didn't know what I was doing in 2016, 2017 or 2018 while I was successful. I was simply searching for something to click and make everything feel normal again. Eventually this led to my shoulder getting inflamed and I missed time.

When I got sent down to AA I sat down with the pitching coach and started watching old film of myself pitching side by side with film of me in AAA. There were a lot of differences. We started working before the game during catch on getting my body back into positions that I was successful in. It felt weird at first but after a couple days I started feeling more natural. I finished the season throwing really well and won Southern League Reliever of the Month the last month of the season. I tell this story because everyone is going to struggle, lose feel for a pitch, or even just flat out pitch bad for whatever reason. Being able to fix something on your own and fast is a big key to being successful. The faster you can make adjustments, the more consistent you will be and the more success you will have. Sometimes these adjustments happen outing to outing, inning to inning, hitter to hitter, or even pitch to pitch. Being able to make mechanical notes or checkpoints will help to make adjustments easier. With that being said, learn yourself and be your own coach. **The only coach you will have from day 1 until the end of your career is yourself.**

Homer Bush

'98 World Series Championship- New York Yankees

Looking back at the '98 World Series, here's what I found really cool: we won a lot of games, won the World Series pretty handedly, but we never got COMFORTABLE. We were always **grinding**. I learned a valuable lesson to just work hard and stay focused all the way until the end— let the dust settle.

Justin Friedman

Consistency is not Conditional

Consistent action is one of the most essential components of success. Some people feel like they have discipline when everything is going well (their body feels good, their home life is in order, and they are in an ideal environment), but then they "lose" it when things go wrong. Consistency, however, is not conditional. Discipline means doing what you are supposed to do regardless of the outside circumstances. To be clear, this does not mean that what you are experiencing is invalid or that the obstacles you run into are imaginary (though at times they can be). Rather, it means that nothing can stand in your way because your will triumphs over whatever you are currently feeling and/ or dealing with. Fortunately, this is a skill that can be developed in other areas of your life. If you do not know where to start, start by making your bed. There will be days that it is easy, days where you are tired, and days where you are in a rush. **The practice of making**

271

your bed every day as soon as you wake up sets the tone and sets you up for success. Not only does it emphasize gratitude for the things you have and foster an attention to detail, but when you wake up and handle the first thing on your to-do list regardless of how you feel you have also built momentum to execute on your other tasks that day. Discipline is a mundane practice and it will go largely unnoticed; it's not flashy, you can't post it on Instagram, but it just works.

Darren Fenster

Tweet

↻ You Retweeted

Darren Fenster
@CoachYourKids

If you're fortunate enough to play in college, you will get your ass handed to you. Playing professionally, the same thing will happen. This is fact.

Train at a level that forces you to fail. You'll have to learn the valuable skill of figuring it out before you actually have to.

"Train at a level that forces you to fail."

HERE'S WHAT DARREN FENSTER, BOSTON RED SOX MINOR LEAGUE OUTFIELD AND BASERUNNING COORDINATOR, HAS TO SAY ABOUT PLAYING AT THE HIGHER LEVELS…

@COACHYOURKIDS

Reaching Home Plate

One thing I learned throughout this book-writing journey is that the baseball community is so open and sharing! It's incredible to see how many great coaches and resources want to share their insights and knowledge. All of those coaches seem to have one common goal: player development. Thank you to all of the contributors who made this book possible.

My hope is that at least one person who reads this takes at least one thing away with them. Putting this together has been one of the greatest experiences of my life so far. From having a boatload of great conversations over Zoom/phone calls, to creating my own website, and to writing and sharing my personal experiences—this has been a humbling journey.

Obviously, I, a former DIII baseball player did not perform to the best of my ability or reach my full potential, but that doesn't mean you or your kid won't unlock it. If I could go back to the first day that I picked up a bat, I would. I would do it over and over and over again. When I advise others to truly cherish every moment the game gives you, I mean it.

My other wish is that I inspired someone to be a 1% better version of themself— whether that be for baseball purposes or in life. As I've mentioned earlier, baseball has turned me into the best version of myself. From my first experience of picking up a baseball, to throwing my last pitch, and to writing my own personal journey in this book, I can certainly conclude that baseball is the greatest sport to ever be played. From first base— to second— to third— and finally, to home plate. I hope you reach home plate: **your full potential**.

REACHING HOME PLATE

CONTRIBUTOR LIST

College Players

Matt Barnes- Shenandoah University

Joe Colucci- Emerson College

Andrea Dalatri- Old Dominion University

Gianluca Dalatri- UNC Chapel Hill

Ty Dudley- Oklahoma Christian University

Nick Cassano- Montclair State University

Joe Duffy- University of Sciences

Mikey Wynne- Brookdale Community College

Pat Reilly- Vanderbilt University

Jack Harnisch- Fordham University

Jake Lawrie- Marist College

Sal Monticiollo- La Salle University

REACHING HOME PLATE

CONTRIBUTOR LIST

College Coaches

Dan Drullinger-Pitching Coach – Cerro Coso Community College

George Brown- Pitching Coach- St. John's University

George Capen- Assistant Coach/ Recruiting Coordinator- The College of the Holy Cross

Gary Trottier- Pitching Coach & Recruiting Coordinator- Lasell University

Victor Diaz- Assistant Coach- Embry-Riddle Aeronautical University

Richard Croushore- Pitching Coach- Shenandoah University- Former MLB player for 11 years

Jason Stein- Assistant/Hitting Coach- Duke University

Tommy Winterstein- Assistant Coach- University of Toledo

Cale Hennemann- Assistant Coach- Belmont University

TJ Ward- Assistant Coach- Ramapo College

Nick Weisheipl- Head Coach- Cabrini University

REACHING HOME PLATE

CONTRIBUTOR LIST
Professional Players

Homer Bush- Former 7 Year MLB Veteran
Pete Harnisch- Former 14 Year MLB Veteran
Brandon Martorano- San Francisco Giants Organization
Josh Tols- Philadelphia Phillies Organization
Sam McMillan- Detroit Tigers Organization
Andre Nnebe- Milwaukee Brewers Organization
Brad Case- Pittsburgh Pirates Organization
Tommy Eveld- Miami Marlins Organization
Alan Trejo- Colorado Rockies Organization
Justin Friedman- Chicago White Sox Organization
Hayden Wesneski- New York Yankees Organization

REACHING HOME PLATE

CONTRIBUTOR LIST
S&C/ Mobility

Gerry DeFilippo- Strength & Sports Performance Coach- Owner of Challenger Strength

Ryan Faer- Performance Coordinator- Cleveland Indians

Nunzio Signore- Strength & Conditioning Coach- Owner of Rockland Peak Performance

Connor Rooney- High Performance Trainer- Driveline Baseball

Tom Kalieta- Strength & Conditioning Coach- Owner of SWEAT

Joseph Potts- Owner of Top Speed Strength & Conditioning. Head of KC Royals Scout Team S&C

Bill Miller- Strength & Conditioning Specialist

Sean Light- CEO of 4A Health- Former Strength Coach for Los Angeles Lakers & Arizona Diamondbacks

CONTRIBUTOR LIST

Hitting

Jordan Stouffer- MiLB Hitting Coach- Cincinnati Reds

Trey Hannam- MiLB Hitting Coach- New York Mets

Donegal Fergus- MiLB Hitting Coordinator- Minnesota Twins

Jarret DeHart- MLB Assistant Hitting Coach- Seattle Mariners

Steve Springer- Former 14 Year Professional Baseball- Hitting Instructor- Mental Skills Coach

Trent Otis- MLB/MiLB Hitting Instructor

Brian Pozos- Hitting Coach/Private Instructor

REACHING HOME PLATE

CONTRIBUTOR LIST
Pitching

Dustin Pease- Former Professional Player- Owner of Lokation Nation- Author of "Lokation Nation's Guide to Commanding Locations"

Jono Armold- MiLB Pitching Coordinator- Texas Rangers

Alan Jaeger- Founder of Jaeger Sports

Rob Hill- MiLB Pitching Coordinator- Los Angeles Dodgers

Josh Zeid- MLB Pitching Rehab Coordinator

Nick Sanzeri- MLB/MiLB Pitching Consultant- Pitching Coach- Mission College

Lennon Richards- Director of High Performance- Baseball Development Group

David Aardsma- Former 9 Year MLB Veteran- Toronto Blue Jays Pitching Rehab Coordinator

REACHING HOME PLATE

CONTRIBUTOR LIST

Fielding (IF/OF/C)

Tim DeJohn- MiLB Infield Coach- Baltimore Orioles

Sean Travers-Founder of 64 Club

Darren Fenster- MiLB Outfield and Baserunning Coordinator- Boston Red Sox

Micheal Thomas- MiLB Catching Coordinator- Minnesota Twins

Todd Coburn – The Catching Guy

REACHING HOME PLATE

CONTRIBUTOR LIST
Nutrition/Recovery

Mike Duffy- Certified Personal Trainer- AAHFRP Post Rehab Certified- Owner of Mike Duffy's Personal Training

Carolann Duffy- Certified Personal Trainer- Holistic Life Coach- Owner of Mike Duffy's Personal Training

Thrive Spine & Sports Rehab

References

Cowden, R. G., Crust, L., Jackman, P. C., & Duckett, T. R. (2019). Perfectionism and motivation in sport: The mediating role of mental toughness. *South African Journal of Science, 115*(1/2), 57–63. https://doi-org.ezproxy.montclair.edu/10.17159/sajs.2019/5271

Duckworth, A. (2016). Grit Scale. Retrieved from https://angeladuckworth.com/grit-scale/

Glass, C. R., Spears, C. A., Perskaudas, R., & Kaufman, K. A. (2019). Mindful Sport Performance Enhancement: Randomized Controlled Trial of a Mental Training Program With Collegiate Athletes. *Journal of Clinical Sport Psychology, 13*(4), 609–628.

Gordhamer, S. (2014, March 5). Mindfulness: The Seattle Seahawks' sports psychologist shares why it matters. *Huffington Post*. Retrieved from http://www.huffingtonpost.com

Harding, T. (2020, April 29). Here's who helped Dahl most on path to Majors. Retrieved from https://www.mlb.com/news/david-dahl-family-hitting-coach

Kaufman, K.A., Glass, C.R., & Pineau, T.R. (2016). Mindful sport performance enhancement (MSPE): Development and applications. In A. Baltzell (Ed.), *Mindfulness and performance* (pp. 153–185). New York, NY: Cambridge University Press.

Kutscher, S., Song, Y., Wang, L., Upender, R., & Malow, B. (2013). Validation of a statistical model predicting possible fatigue effect in Major League Baseball. *Sleep, 36*(Abstract Suppl), A408.

Lindsay, R., Spittle, M., & Larkin, P. (2019). The effect of mental imagery on skill performance in sport: A systematic review. *Journal of Science and Medicine in Sport, 22.* doi: 10.1016/j.jsams.2019.08.111

MarinersPR. (2020, May 18). Checking in with Mariners Assistant Hitting Coach Jarret DeHart. Retrieved from https://marinersblog.mlblogs.com/checking-in-with-mariners-assistant-hitting-coach-jarret-dehart-bb41c00c6adc

Wagner, J. (2019, July 9). Justin Verlander: The Astros' Ace and Sleep Guru. Retrieved from https://www.nytimes.com/2019/07/09/sports/baseball/justin-verlander-all-star-sleep.html

ABOUT AUTHOR

Perry Quartuccio is currently a student at Montclair State University. Perry is aiming to earn his undergraduate degree in Psychology and seeking to go to graduate school to earn a degree in Sports Psychology. Perry aspires to become a mental performance coach (CMPC) and hopes to work in professional baseball.

Twitter: @PerryQuartuccio Instagram: @_perryquartuccio

www.reachinghomeplate.com